T5-AQA-672

PALGRAVE Studies in Oral History

Series Editors: Linda Shopes and Bruce M. Stave

I Saw it Coming: Worker Narratives of Plant Closings and Job Loss, by Tracy E. K'Meyer and Joy L. Hart (2010)

Speaking History: Oral Histories of the American Past, 1865–Present, by Sue Armitage and Laurie Mercier (2010)

Surviving Bhopal: Dancing Bodies, Written Texts, and Oral Testimonials of Women in the Wake of an Industrial Disaster, by Suroopa Mukherjee (2010)

Living with Jim Crow: African American Women and Memories of the Segregated South, by Leslie Brown and Anne Valk (2010)

Stories from the Gulag, by Jehanne Gheith and Katherine Jolluck (2010)

I Saw It Coming

Worker Narratives of Plant Closings and Job Loss

Tracy E. K'Meyer and Joy L. Hart

palgrave
macmillan

I SAW IT COMING

First published in 2009 by
PALGRAVE MACMILLAN®
in the United States—a division of St. Martin's Press LLC,
175 Fifth Avenue, New York, NY 10010.

Where this book is distributed in the UK, Europe and the rest of the world,
this is by Palgrave Macmillan, a division of Macmillan Publishers Limited,
registered in England, company number 785998, of Houndmills,
Basingstoke, Hampshire RG21 6XS.

Palgrave Macmillan is the global academic imprint of the above companies
and has companies and representatives throughout the world.

Palgrave® and Macmillan® are registered trademarks in the United States,
the United Kingdom, Europe and other countries.

ISBN: 978–1–4039–7745–8

Library of Congress Cataloging-in-Publication Data is available from the
Library of Congress.

A catalogue record of the book is available from the British Library.

Design by Newgen Imaging Systems (P) Ltd., Chennai, India.

First edition: December 2009

10 9 8 7 6 5 4 3 2 1

Printed in the United States of America.

*To the memory of Jean K'Meyer and
with loving thanks to Jim K'Meyer
and
To Florene L. and Charles H. Hart
with appreciation for lifelong lessons
about work and play*

Contents

Series Editors' Foreword

Long after the Great Depression of the 1930s and long before the severe economic downturn at the conclusion of the first decade of the twenty-first century, workers across the nation's rustbelt suffered from deindustrialization. Plant closings became commonplace as jobs moved to cheaper labor markets at home or abroad. This study, based on the oral histories of sixteen workers in Louisville, Kentucky's International Harvester (IH) and Johnson Controls (JC) factories that shut down during the 1980s and 1990s, respectively, transcends that locality to reveal a general portrait of the impact of deindustrialization on individuals, families, and communities.

The volume is organized by subject, not individual biographies, so that personal stories of the interviewees appear throughout all of the chapters. This permits the authors to cover a variety of work-related topics including narratives that discuss how workers obtained their jobs, the nature of work at IH and JC, the process of the closings, their impact on the workers, and the lessons learned from the experience. Job loss is always difficult, and in the words of one worker, "It was almost like an airplane crash. You don't prepare when you get on a plane for it to crash. It happens . . . , and that's pretty much the way that was." While, perhaps, they were not prepared, workers had distinct ideas about the cause of plant closings. They frequently cited bad management and, in the case of the Johnson Controls shutdown during the 1990s, jobs lost to the North American Free Trade Agreement (NAFTA), which made it easier for foreign companies to sell in U.S. markets. While interviewees may have been victims of economic policies that led to job loss, the oral histories clearly showed they exerted agency in ways that permitted them to mitigate poor shop floor conditions. Overall, the narratives reveal the complexity of their experience, and the ambivalence they felt about the loss of a job on the one hand and the release it offered for new life opportunities on the other.

From the perspective of oral history methodology, the authors pursued an unusual approach. Joy Hart, an expert in organizational communication, conducted a general interview that began with the very open-ended question, "Can you tell me about your job?" This often elicited a great deal of information about health, safety, and working conditions. Two weeks later, Tracy K'Meyer, an oral historian, followed by asking more specific questions about the interviewee's personal history—their family background and life outside of work. The combined synthesis of the two sessions provided a broad array of information that permitted the book to be organized in its final form. By providing the narrators the opportunity to elaborate on their working lives and reactions to plant closings, the authors confirm their assertion that oral history adds the complexity of human experience to the generally one-dimensional story of deindustrialization.

This volume, the latest in the Palgrave Studies in Oral History series, joins two other books, Sandy Polishuk's *Sticking to the Union* (2003) and Jane LaTour's *Sisters in the Brotherhoods* (2008), that focus upon work and workers. Other themes in the series include African Americans and desegregation, women's history, and major events outside of the borders of the United States such as the Holocaust, China's Cultural Revolution, Argentina's "dirty war," and the upheaval of Iraq's last Jews. In bringing these and other subjects to print, we continue our effort to publish the best in oral history for scholars, students, and the general reader.

Bruce M. Stave
University of Connecticut

Linda Shopes
Carlisle, Pennsylvania

Acknowledgments

Without the cooperation and enthusiasm of the interviewees, this project would have been impossible. We thank them for sharing their time, their stories, and their insights with us and for allowing us to share these with a broader audience. We also thank the Kentucky Oral History Commission and the University of Louisville for providing funding critical to completing this book. In addition, several other individuals provided vital assistance during the project. Several unions, as well as past and current officials, facilitated recruiting interviewees. Jefferson Cowie and Joseph Heathcott helped us refine ideas in an earlier essay on this material. Further, we greatly enjoyed working with Linda Shopes and Bruce Stave at Palgrave. They provided helpful feedback and quick responses throughout the process.

Tracy K'Meyer thanks A. Glenn Crothers—husband, colleague, and editor—for being a sounding board and source of moral support throughout this project and all her work. Joy Hart also thanks her family and friends—two- and four-legged—for their support and encouragement. They made the project both more rewarding and more fun.

Introduction

In 1997 when Joy Hart interviewed Rob McQueen, a former employee of the International Harvester plant in Louisville, Kentucky, McQueen struggled to explain how he felt about losing his job, saying:

> Whoever listens to this will think I'm nuts. I have so many mixed emotions on it. When Harvester shut down, I was devastated but yet—God, I was so happy. It was just such a hell but, yet, it was my income, it was my life. I was overjoyed, I was sad, I was hurt. Every emotion that you can feel, I think I went through it. I was relieved because I didn't have to work like that. I was hurt and sad because I was losing a lot of friends. I was losing a lot of my benefits, insurance and what have you. But, at the same time, I was almost happy. I know that doesn't make sense.... I'm glad that I don't still work there, but, man, I wish I still worked there. Does that make sense to you?

He continued in the course of two multi-hour recording sessions to describe the brutal heat and pressure of the workplace, his talent and reliability on the job, and the process of losing his livelihood when the company shut its doors. In doing so he made clear not only why he was happy to lose the job—the unbearable conditions that left him with permanent scars—but what he saw as the reasons for the shutdown and the long-term impact on himself and others. His emotional struggle to convey his perspective to the interviewers and the imagined larger audience for his story highlighted not only the personal difficulty of trying to summarize one's own story, but also the complexity of workers' experiences and memories of deindustrialization.

Stories of plant closings such as the one McQueen experienced have become commonplace in both the popular media and scholarly publications. As deindustrialization spread across the country, news coverage and popular press writings chronicled the stranglehold on many factories and communities.[1] The initial wave of studies of this phenomenon focused primarily on the large-scale social and economic consequences. By employing surveys and statistics this work produced aggregate data on general trends and responses, but told us little about the experiences of individual workers displaced by job loss.[2] When workers were invited to speak for themselves in news reports or quotes to support survey findings, only small sections of their stories were used and these were typically employed for dramatic effect—to highlight the anguish and resentment associated with plant closings. In short, former employees were rarely allowed to reflect on the causes, process, or meaning of deindustrialization.[3] While these reports of plant closings did address shifts in the national economy and types of labor as well as impacts on communities devastated by loss of major employers, they obscured the effects on individuals and the responses of the working class.

In the past twenty years scholars from a range of disciplines have employed ethnographic methods of participant observation and extended interviews to explore deindustrialization from a grassroots perspective. An early example was *Rusted Dreams: Hard Times in a Steel Community*, in which David Bensman and Roberta Lynch combine a portrait of a south Chicago neighborhood with a call to action to prevent such devastation from recurring in other communities. Scholars have used personal narrative not only to give firsthand views of events and their results but to draw conclusions about the nature of work and worker identity. Kathryn Marie Dudley, for example, in *End of the Line: Lost Jobs, New Lives in Postindustrial America*, sees in the individual stories of the death of an automobile factory a larger transition in the nature of work from a "culture of hand" to a "culture of mind." In a comparative study of the decline of the steel industry in the United States and Canada, Steven High likewise uses personal narratives to illustrate the differing responses on the part of workers on either side of the border, and how that was shaped by national identity. The theme of the collective memory of deindustrialization and its meaning for communities has begun to emerge in this literature, reflecting a broader interest in memory and commemoration in the academy. Thus in *Steeltown USA: Work and Memory in Youngstown*, Sherry Lee Linkon and John Russo employ a variety of texts, including oral histories, to demonstrate how the rise and fall of steel is represented in the collective consciousness of the people of Youngstown, Ohio. Much of this work, drawing as it does on life stories of the displaced, allows readers to begin to understand the experiences of the workers, to view the impact of deindustrialization from their perspective, and to consider the personal and communal meaning of events through the lens of memory. But, because most of this literature is in the form of traditional monographs, the dominant voice is that of the scholar; at times individual workers are not named, and at others they are represented as composite characters or only quoted in brief selections as evidence for the author's argument.[4]

Using combinations of oral history and photography, in recent years scholars have experimented with moving away from the monograph format, in order to present, as Michael Frisch describes his contribution, a portrait of the workers that allows relatively unmediated access to their experience. Frisch's *Portraits in Steel*, with photographs by Milton Rogovin, contains edited transcripts of interviews with steelworkers in Buffalo, New York, and aims to allow the men and women to present themselves to the reader with both their posed images and their stories. In similar fashion, historian Thomas Dublin and photographer George Harvan document the stories of residents of the anthracite coal regions of Pennsylvania in *When the Mines Closed: Stories of Struggles in Hard Times*. In both cases Dublin and Frisch provide an introduction that gives a short historical background and context for the interviews, but choose to refrain from extended analysis, though Dublin goes further in laying out the themes he sees in the interviews.[5]

Contemporaneous with Dublin's work, Judith Modell and Charlee Brodsky released *Town without Steel: Envisioning Homestead*, which likewise employs visual images and personal narratives to bring the story of that community to readers, but also includes a longer opening chapter of interpretation and commentary. In the recent volume *Corporate Wasteland: The Landscape and Memory of Deindustrialization*, historian Steven High and photographer David W. Lewis combine analytical essays, photographs, and the voices of workers to examine the effects of deindustrialization and the transnational forces affecting it. With this approach, High and Lewis blend elements of the edited oral history collection with the interpretive work of the monograph, making the book an experiment in bringing different voices—of both those who experienced deindustrialization and those who study them—into conversation. The idea of conversation is also modeled by the authors of *"I Was Content and Not Content": The Story of Linda Lord and the Closing of Penobscot Poultry*, in which extended excerpts of the interview with Lord are combined with photographs and interpretive essays from a number of scholars. In each of these works, the story of deindustrialization's impact on individuals and communities is presented in lengthy edited oral histories, allowing the reader to "hear" firsthand the workers' experiences. To the extent practical in a written text of necessarily limited length the language of the workers is preserved, so that they are telling their own stories in their own words and readers can make their own interpretations of these histories.[6]

Extending these latter models, we hope in this volume to welcome the reader into a conversation, among the workers primarily but including our voice and interpretation as well, about the experience of work and deindustrialization in two plants in Louisville, Kentucky. In doing so we seek both to convey workers' self-presentation and interpretation of their stories and to fulfill our responsibility as scholars to draw meaning from the narratives. Oral histories do not stand alone as simple statements about the past but in fact are heavily mediated and constructed documents that convey stories shaped by the circumstances under which they are created. We as scholars chose the subject, selected the workers who then had the opportunity to share their perspectives, asked the questions, and provided an immediate audience about whom the narrators likely had preconceived notions—young, female, middle class, with no industrial experience. As important, in the end, we selected the excerpts, edited them, and arranged them in this volume. At the same time, the workers chose how to answer the questions. Most made it very clear that they recognized they were speaking to a larger unseen audience, and in fact appeared to relish the opportunity to pass their interpretation of events—and advice—on to later generations. In short, they told their story as they want that future audience to understand it. Put another way, borrowing from Frisch and Rogovin, they presented their autobiography, experience of work, understanding of the causes of deindustrialization, and interpretation of its personal and societal impact in their own terms. In this volume we sought to allow the narrators to speak with a minimum of introductory historical background and context, and then to add our voice to the conversation in a concluding chapter.[7]

In order to explore questions of how deindustrialization affects workers and their families, and how they understand and explain plant closings, we identified three businesses in and near Louisville, Kentucky: International Harvester, which closed its doors in the mid-1980s, Johnson Controls, which shut down in the early 1990s, and M. Fine and Sons, a shirt manufacturing facility just across the river in Indiana that had closed a year before our study. Our intention was to compare the experience in three industries across nearly three decades to see if and how it differed. We began with Johnson Controls because Joy Hart had met some laid-off employees through her volleyball league and had become intrigued by their stories. Indeed, the genesis of the project was Hart's desire to understand what had happened to these men and women, both as a scholar of workplace communication—how workers share their stories—and as a friend. Harvester was an obvious choice because it had been one of the largest single industrial employers in the community. We selected M. Fine because it had closed so recently. Ultimately, we had to drop the garment facility from the study because we found too few interviewees to make a reasonable sample.

We chose Louisville because it is our home and we wanted to explore the impact of these economic changes in our own community. Tracy K'Meyer's interest in part stemmed from a desire to augment the archival collections of oral histories about the Louisville metropolitan area. But the location had the benefit of contributing new insights to the existing literature in two ways. First, at the time when most of these narrators entered the working world and when the plants closed, Louisville had a relatively mixed economy with a wide variety of small- and large manufacturers. It was not dependent on one large employer, and thus could form a contrast with the literature that focuses on the decline of a major industry or large-scale employer, such as steel or automobile production. The project's multiple plant approach reflects this mixed industry setting. Second, its geographic location in the upper South provides an alternative view in a literature dominated by the rust belt and upper Midwest. Louisville has previously been the subject of one comparative study of the response to deindustrialization, *The Politics of Plant Closings*, by John Portz. Portz focused, however, on the actions of civic leaders and the political response. Our study complements this work and brings the insider perspective of the workers themselves.[8]

The Louisville economy was tied to commerce and manufacturing almost from the beginning. In the 1800s the city was a hub for transportation systems between both east and west and north and south first because of its location on the Ohio River and later as a railroad center. Although that role declined after the Civil War when Cincinnati built a competing rail line, the city's economy remained focused on commerce and increasingly on industry as local citizens launched the first wave of manufacturing enterprises, mainly small and local and aimed at the southern market. After World War I the city joined the nationwide boom of the roaring 1920s, as Louisvillians opened over 150 new manufacturing facilities employing over 36,000 people by the end of the decade. This development included the Ford Motor Company, which built its first plant in 1914 and expanded it in 1925.[9]

The period of national crises during the Great Depression and World War II was relatively kind to Louisville, by the end triggering a dramatic acceleration in economic growth and industrialization in the city. While Louisvillians shared the hard times caused by high unemployment and bank failures after the stock market crash that triggered the Depression, the city was buffered to some extent by continuing demand for one of its major products—tobacco—and increased consumption of another—alcohol. Indeed, the end of Prohibition helped to cause a minor economic boom in the city by 1937. It was the massive industrial effort accompanying World War II that made the most significant impact on Louisville, however. Even before the United States formally entered the war, defense industries and facilities, such as the powder plant and naval ordinance center in nearby southern Indiana and more importantly the rubber and chemical industry in the western neighborhoods of Louisville, created an 18 percent rise in industrial employment by spring 1940. During the war, as more local plants converted to military production, employment in manufacturing reached a peak of 80,000 men and women. Though focused on defense production, many of these businesses either remained in operation after the war, or the facilities were converted into peacetime production by other firms.[10]

The industrial expansion continued after World War II and through the next three decades. Between 1940 and 1970 manufacturing accounted for 42 percent of the increased employment in the Louisville metropolitan area, creating approximately 53,000 jobs. According to census figures, by 1950, 31 percent of the city's employed population worked in manufacturing, a figure that remained almost the same for 1960 and 1970. This boom was part of a wave of southern industrialization, fueled by the rise of branch plants of large national firms that moved into the region to tap the postwar wealth of its inhabitants. In Louisville this expansion included the largest employer in the city, General Electric, as well as other "corporate giants" such as B. F. Goodrich and Anaconda Aluminum. International Harvester joined this migration in 1946 when it bought the Curtiss-Wright airplane plant and converted it to produce farm tractors. At the same time, large numbers of smaller firms also set up shop, giving Louisville a diverse industrial base. For example, in 1956 the Globe Union Company of Milwaukee—later bought by Johnson Controls, Inc.—opened a small facility employing one hundred people producing batteries. According to Chamber of Commerce president Kenneth P. Vinsel, this company was one of seventeen in just one year to start "pilot" facilities with the possibility of expansion later in the community. The result of this growth was a period of high employment and diverse options for people seeking manufacturing jobs, just at the time when many of the narrators in this volume were embarking on their work careers.[11]

By the end of the 1970s, however, there were signs of a downturn in manufacturing in the Louisville area, a trend that would continue into the ensuing decades and include the shutdown of both International Harvester and Johnson Controls. Louisville again reflected national patterns, in this case the decline of American industry that began in the rust belt and urban north and spread across the country. Between 1974 and 1978 alone Louisville and Jefferson County lost 9,500 manufacturing jobs. The decade saw downsizing at some of the largest firms, including General Electric, which went from a peak of 23,000 workers to 15,000. Harvester shared in this belt-tightening, cutting its workforce from its high point of 6,500 to 4,000. During this slowdown in 1978 Globe Union sold the Louisville facility to Johnson Controls, Inc. The diminishing of the manufacturing base of the local economy continued into the 1980s as some of the city's largest manufacturers began closing their doors. In 1979 the Brown and Williamson Tobacco Corporation ceased production in the city, though it maintained a white-collar workforce at its downtown headquarters. Soon thereafter American Standard, Seagram's, Lorillard Tobacco, and finally International Harvester shut their plants. As a result by the mid-1980s manufacturing employment in the county had dropped another 17 percent. Some of these losses were offset by a rise in white-collar and service-oriented employment in downtown financial and other enterprises, as Louisville made a transition to a postindustrial economy. Yet the overall unemployment rate still reached 8.3 percent.

The Louisville economy rebounded somewhat in the 1990s, but by the end of the century the movement away from a manufacturing base had proceeded. In 1998 the U.S. Department of Commerce issued a report listing the community as one of several rebounding rust-belt cities because its economy had seen a 4.7 percent growth and unemployment had fallen to 4.4 percent. The decade had brought a rise in new business starts and even the creation of over 7,000 manufacturing jobs. This growth appeared to be a last hurrah for industrial expansion, however, as over the next few years those gains quickly and dramatically reversed. In the five years after 1998 the community saw a 9.5 percent decrease in manufacturing employment, and by mid-decade a total of 16,900 jobs were lost. This late 1990s downturn, coming as it did in the aftermath of the 1994 adoption of the North American Free Trade Agreement (NAFTA), set the context for the interviews, and thus likely colored not only the narrators' outlook of their own future prospects but their views of the economy as a whole.[12]

For our study we interviewed twenty-four men and women, although in the process of preparing this collection we narrowed our base to sixteen people, seven former employees of International Harvester and nine from Johnson Controls. At the time of the interviews, some of these former employees had retired, others were in school, and some had launched new careers, usually making less money than they were at these factories. We identified the first interviewees through Hart's social ties. In addition, we were able to contact some narrators through union officials and meetings. Both International Harvester and Globe Union were unionized and closed shop facilities before any of our narrators started working there. The United Auto Workers was the dominant union in each facility, though there were a number of smaller unions such as the machinists and electrical workers present at Harvester. Although all the narrators just by being employed were union members, they displayed a range of attachment from those who served as long-time officers and for whom it was a primary identification to others for whom membership was a formality only. The union presidents in the plants at the time of the closings assisted us in recruiting participants and allowed us to speak to meetings of "alumni." Finally, and most fruitfully, once we started talking to former employees they suggested other people, and our list snowballed.

As in any oral history project, our methods for identifying and contacting narrators influenced the types of stories we heard. Our primary means of making contact, social networks and activity in union meetings, produced a sample loaded with people who likely shared similar outlooks and situations—that is why they are friends—and those with an attachment to the union and presumably the values of cooperation and solidarity that that implies. Just their ability and willingness to participate indicates that the narrators were or saw themselves as survivors, as people who landed on their feet. They had phones so we could contact them, homes they were willing to invite us into, and time to spend with us. There was a range of experiences, however, as some of the older, more infirm interviewees were having more of a financial and personal struggle at the time of our meetings. These, and other narrators, may have been motivated by the opportunity to air grievances. Two notes should be made of who is not in the sample. Those who left the community are not heard from here. In part, our original goals included documenting the impact of deindustrialization on this community, requiring narrators who could speak to the experience in Louisville after the closing. Moreover, people who left fell out of the social network and were less likely to be identified as potential narrators. Finally, all the narrators who are in this volume are white. While a few African Americans attended the union alumni meetings, none volunteered to be interviewed, and none of the referrals led to African Americans. We did interview one black nurse at Harvester, but as an educated professional she was eliminated from the book because her experience was an outlier. The few other professionals interviewed also are not included. In follow-up interviews we asked each narrator about race relations in the plant, and thus that material is in the transcripts in the archives, but because that did not arise as an organic theme in the stories we chose not to focus on it here.

To record the stories of these workers, we employed a two-phase interview process. Initially, Joy Hart conducted broad, general interviews. The goal of these initial interviews was to give the narrators wide latitude to tell their stories as they wanted; thus, she engaged them in open, flowing, informal conversation and allowed their experiences to spill forth. Hart asked interviewees only a few open-ended questions such as "What was working in the plant like?" and "How did the closing affect you?" and then let them talk at length, uninterrupted, as well as to digress as they saw fit. Although she probed and asked follow-up questions at times, she tried to minimize these in this round of interviewing, encouraging the narrator to tell his/her story and recording it as it emerged.

Approximately two weeks after each initial interview, Tracy K'Meyer met with the narrator for a second session. She developed a specific interview guide for each interview after reviewing the tape recording of the initial meeting. Often narrators would describe their work tasks and conditions in ways that assumed knowledge on the part of the listener, leaving sections of the initial interview hard to follow. K'Meyer's task was to prompt the narrators to explain these parts further. The second goal of these follow-up interviews was to establish a personal context for the events surrounding the closing. She asked about the narrator's family background, prior work history, marriage, children, and involvement in social activities. Because these interviews were meant to be archival resources as well as material for our own work, in the second session K'Meyer covered broader themes such as race relations in the workplace, union activism, and local economic conditions. This two-phased interviewing process resulted in approximately four to five hours of taped conversation for each interviewee, with about half of this time in the first interview and half in the second.

Since Hart is a scholar of organizational communication and K'Meyer is an historian, we had the opportunity to compare the methods of interviewing and editing in our respective disciplines. When interviewing we both listened for powerful quotes, consistencies and inconsistencies in the narrator's story, areas needing further questioning, and emerging themes. In constructing the interview guide, we had to determine how to combine the oral history interview approach that includes questions aimed at documenting personal history, such as family background and life outside of work, with that of organizational communication, which focuses more exclusively on workplace experiences and employee viewpoints related to their jobs. For the most part, we chose to use the broader life approach of oral history. This focus ensured that narrators would talk about their paths to these factory jobs, their work itself, reactions to and insights on the closings, and experiences during and after the shutdowns. This way the narratives would include early-life assumptions about work, descriptions of life on the job, and reflections on work and life after the closing as well as subsequent jobs. This prioritizing of the oral history approach likewise guided the transcribing, editing, and presentation of the material in these chapters.[13]

After transcription of the interviews, we began the editing process by reading each other's interviews. During this phase, we became more familiar with all of the stories and began correcting transcription errors. Once these initial transcript reviews were completed we deposited the interviews in the Oral History Collection of the University of Louisville archives, where they are available for public use. We began preparing the narratives for this volume by identifying key topics and themes. We chose to present the story in a relatively chronological series of chapters focused on the subjects of getting the job, the nature of work in the plants, the process of the closing, the personal impact, and finally the lessons the narrators learned from the experience. Each chapter is introduced briefly by setting the context and highlighting a few key themes. We chose to otherwise restrict commentary until the final chapter to allow the reader to be drawn into the workers' stories and perspectives.

Readers of this volume should be aware of our practices in the editing and presentation of the material. We chose to break from the more typical approach of focusing the chapters on individuals—a person per chapter—and instead to organize the book according to the process of getting the job, work, losing the job, and the aftermath. The consequence of this decision is that the personal stories are cut up, sacrificing the intimacy of the autobiographical approach. But, we hope that sacrifice is outweighed by the benefits of setting up a dialogue among the workers on each of the key topics. In order to preserve some of the biographical approach we begin with a chapter introducing each narrator's prior life story, and favored relatively long excerpts where possible. The juxtaposition of narrative segments on workplace conditions, expectations of work, and other topics also highlighted thematic consistency across the interviews. As in any published volume of oral histories, space constraints forced the cutting of large amounts from each interview. Moreover, in this case there were two versions of each person's story, and in the effort to combine them some repetitive material had to be dropped. We sought to take segments from each of the two interview sessions and merge them in ways that produced the most complete account. Here we sought a balance between the organizational communication preference for preserving the original structure and the historians' interest in arranging the material into a chronologically or thematically coherent narrative. We also eliminated the interviewers' questions and responses, and nonrelated asides such as offers of refreshments and discussions about the weather. In part this decision was a space-saving one and followed the model of many, if not most, collections of oral histories. More important, because material from two interviews was combined and the narratives were divided by theme rather than by the original order of the conversation, reinserting questions would create in many cases a false rendering of the exchange. Finally, at times the narrators assumed the listener had certain knowledge and left some parts of their stories unelaborated or implicit. As a result, as we integrated the material and tried to construct the narratives in a manner that made the resulting story most comprehensible to readers, we had to add connecting or clarifying words and phrases in some places.

In the course of their interviews, these narrators chose topics to emphasize, gave their own interpretations of events, and drew conclusions from their experience alone and in comparison with others. As scholars we mold these stories into the form that ends up on the published page. But, although that by itself is an intervention and a case of sharing authorship with the narrators, it still falls short of fulfilling our responsibility.[14] We must also join the conversation with our own conclusions, drawn from the interviews as a group. As oral historians, folklorists, and others who examine personal narratives have noted, by examining the recurring content, themes, and ways of organizing a narrative in a body of qualitative autobiographical evidence, we can begin to understand the collective story, especially how it reflects individual and community consciousness, identity, and values.[15] In this case, it was clear that certain topics took unanticipated dominance in the narratives, common motifs arose in how the workers explained themselves, and inconsistencies and contradictions both between and within interviews demanded an explanation.

Although we reserve our more detailed analysis for the concluding chapter in order to avoid overly predetermining the reader's encounter with the narratives, we must acknowledge the themes we identified in the interviews, which informed our selection of the stories and arrangement of the chapters. These themes serve as a guide for readers to the conversation presented here. An interpretative essay elaborating on these themes follows the narratives in the concluding chapter. The narrators were proud of the hard work demanded in their jobs and their skill at performing it. They describe in detail the health and safety dangers present in their jobs and the challenges associated with working in such conditions, and stress that in order to perform well one must possess skill, intelligence, and a strong work ethic. A related theme was their feeling of being owed respect from management because they worked hard, possessed skill and commitment, and produced a quality product in these trying conditions. This respect was not afforded them, however, causing resentment and alienation. Although in some cases they acknowledge a host of other factors, these interviewees put the blame for the plant closures squarely on poor management and government actions (e.g., NAFTA). With a few exceptions, despite citing numerous examples of financial, psychological, and personal hardship they suffered during and after the plant closings, these narrators maintain that they would not go back to work at these companies and are happier with their current jobs and lives.

Of particular interest across these narratives is the ambivalence sometimes displayed by the interviewees, as evidenced by the internal contradictions in their stories. They spoke of disappointment, anger, and resentment, but also stressed that they were happier since the closings. They disclosed worries about retirement, difficulties finding good paying jobs, and cutting back expenses, but they also maintained that they did not want to go back to factory work, especially in these plants. Sometimes they acknowledged their conflicting feelings and views; most often they did not. This ambivalence can inform us about worker responses to plant closings as well as how individuals make sense of difficult life experiences. Thus these stories, while revealing much about coping with job loss in plant closings, also shed light on how people struggle to preserve a positive self-image and to emphasize perseverance in surmounting challenges, integrating these facets of life into a positive overall view—or put more simply, into a happy ending.

CHAPTER I

"This Plant's Going to Be There Forever"

In this chapter the men and women who worked at and eventually lost their jobs in the closings of the International Harvester and Johnson Controls plants explain how they came to be employed in these enterprises. Their stories were shaped by two contexts: the expectations they had growing up in the working-class neighborhoods of Louisville and the opportunities in the local economy at the time they entered the workforce. In the words of Rob McQueen, most of them were "South End" boys (and girls), a reference to the expanding white, working-class suburb in the southern end of the city and county made up of neighborhoods such as Fairdale, Pleasure Ridge Park, and Valley Station. Growth in these areas resulted both from migration out of rural Kentucky and white flight from inner-city neighborhoods. The recent roots in agriculture and blue-collar jobs of this community are reflected in the family histories of these narrators. Family and neighborhood connections in local industrial plants also informed their expectations for their own careers.

Most of these narrators took their jobs at International Harvester and Johnson Controls between 1957 and 1970, with most of them starting in the late 1960s. This was a time of declining unemployment and increasing industrial opportunity in the community, with the unemployment rate reaching a low in 1969 of 2.8 percent. Indeed, during this period, unemployment in the city was consistently lower than the national average. Jobs were relatively plentiful in part due to the variety of manufacturing firms, which numbered 850 at the end of the decade and were adding an average of over 3,000 jobs a year.[1] Abundant industrial employment opportunities, thus, gave these workers a sense of having options and the ability to make a choice in their career.

Don Anderson, International Harvester

At about seventeen my dad went to work as an electrical helper. He helped to wire some houses. He said it wasn't long, a week or two, and he could run the whole job. So he started doing electrical work and he always liked it. But, he also worked as an automobile mechanic. Then he owned a service station. The land that the service station was on, it was being leased. They sold the lease out from under him and he had to close up. He didn't go back into the service station business. It was pretty tough holding down two jobs. He had got out of electrical work to be an automobile mechanic and then he went back into the electrical because it actually paid more than being an automobile mechanic back then. And, work was picking up in the electrical end so he stayed into it.

During the Second World War, I fantasized that I would be an Air Force pilot or a bomber or something and I fantasized being a priest. I just had all these ideas. Then when I graduated from grade school and went into high school, well I was being bombarded with "What do you want to do?" I had all these ideas but I just never did put them together. Already by then I was doing wiring around the house, since I was about fifteen or sixteen. Dad would supervise it but I would do all the work. He'd get home from work and then look it over. Mother wouldn't let me hook it up. She wouldn't let me torch the house down, but he'd come in and hook it up for me after he checked it over. So I gained a little confidence there before I even graduated from high school.

I knew I was good with my hands but I always kind of felt like it was electrical I wanted. I waited 'til my senior year before I finally decided that that's what I wanted to be. I knew the next forty years was going to be drudgery if you didn't pick something that you enjoyed doing. I feel like if you get some enjoyment out of certain things, then pick along those lines. Otherwise you might have a hard time getting to work. So I finally in my senior year decided that's where I wanted to head. I had some others trying to talk me into going to college so I was on the fence there for a while. But then I decided well, college is just not for me. I think more of a trade school would be the best for me.

Dad said he would help me, so he helped me to get on as a helper and he told me, "From now on it's up to you. You're going to have to learn and keep up with it." Right out of high school I went to work for Link Electric as a helper and then after about a year and a half I went in the service and became an electrician in the Navy. When I got out of the service and went into electrical trade school I did apply myself more than in high school. I did fairly well and I kept my grades above an eighty-something. Eighty-two I believe was my final grade. At that time, most of them were a little bit less. I think everybody passed but I ended up—well, myself and four or five others—tutoring some of them because they wasn't able to keep up. I look back and maybe if I'd applied myself a little more, who knows where I'd have been? But that time's past, I'm not going to worry about that.

When I got back [from the service] I still had to serve two more years of my apprenticeship before I got my journeyman's card in '57. With the journeyman's ticket you can make more money and, of course, you're making journeyman's pay instead of helper's pay. Back then it was twice as much. I had the contractor tell me, he says, "Well, I can keep you as a helper but I can't keep you as a journeyman." I said, "Well, then lay me off, I'm gone." I was positive of what I could do. I think I know my limitations, but I was positive I could handle it and I did. I went out and I finally proved to myself and everybody that I could handle it. And so I've been doing it ever since.

There wasn't that much [construction] work around here so I decided to try maintenance at L&N [Railroad]. That didn't work out too well. I wasn't all that happy and wasn't making the money either. I wasn't making quite enough money to meet all our expenses and make the house payment and so forth. I thought this isn't going to get it. I got to find something else. I was doing what they called electrical work on the railroad. But it was more or less like doing more mechanical work than it was electrical. Instead of construction, where you would install, I was doing maintenance. I was maintaining the machines, electrically. But they didn't pay very good. Harvester come along and it was more money. When I first walked in the door it was a dollar more on the hour and that was a sizeable difference back then in '64. And [it was] more electrical work instead of all this mechanical work.

I just sort of fell in [at Harvester] with my background in the Navy and my knowledge of construction. I just sort of fell right in with them out there and they kept me for twenty-two and a half years and then they shut the doors and wouldn't let me back.

Charlie Noyes, Johnson Controls

What did I think I wanted to be? I hadn't the foggiest idea what I wanted to be. As far as choosing an occupation, that was probably, when I was growing up, the farthest thing from my mind. In that day and time, no one counseled you about what you were going to do later on. In high school I took drafting and machine shop. That was a vocational course. That's what prepared me for what I eventually ended up doing.

I was, I guess, mechanically gifted. I could take things apart and put them together. I could repair them. A lot of people in that day and time couldn't. I was curious about everything. You see, when I was five years old or somewhere thereabout, there was a little neighborhood grocery store sat on the corner. I was already interested in electrical things even at that age. I can remember on more than one occasion that if I would get a nickel to get some candy, I'd go buy a battery, flashlight battery. It was a means for me to do something else to discover. I was curious in that field—electricity and electronics, in particular—even at that age.

My first real job probably was in my junior year in high school. I got a job at Wilcox Motor Company helping several other fellows, one who owned a body shop. He was in charge of their used car repair and clean-up details. They hired me for that one summer to clean up and get used cars conditioned for the lot. That was really my first job as I recall. Probably the next year I worked for an auto paint shop, sanding vehicles, masking vehicles, getting them ready for the painter to paint. I worked there one summer. Gee, I had several jobs, I guess. I worked for a glass company that is no longer in existence, mainly as a laborer doing whatever they needed me to do. I worked for Gonason Homes, a prefab home outfit in New Albany, [Indiana], for a period of time.

I graduated from high school in the middle of the Korean War. So here I am, eighteen years old. I looked for a machinist apprenticeship. You couldn't buy one. If you were draft age, there was no way they would talk to you. They weren't interested in training somebody that was going to be siphoned off to the military. So you couldn't for love nor money get an apprenticeship in a machine shop. This relative got me a job at Brown and Williamson Tobacco Company. I lasted there about ten days, I guess. It was a very short job. Being young and dumb, I got put into the most menial of labor jobs, sweeping and mopping floors, etcetera. Didn't mind that at all. That wasn't a problem. Work never bothered me. In the week or two to ten days or whatever I worked there, I had talked to the members of the labor pool I was in. A lot of these guys were old fellows near retirement, probably none of which were well educated or suited for a different position. I got to asking some of these fellows, "How long you been here?" Some of them had been there twenty, twenty-five years. I thought, "No way, Jose. I ain't cut out for mopping floors the rest of my life." I thought to myself, "This is not the kind of a place I want to work at." I simply left there.

I got on at American Tobacco. First thing they put me to doing was boxing up cartons of cigarettes in cases. I worked at that for a while. It wasn't long before they decided they'd make a machine operator out of me. Trained me for a week with a machine operator and gave me a machine of my own to operate. I spent seventeen and a half years there before they closed it down. By the time they shut it down, I had worked my way up into the maintenance of the machine and was really just beginning to get good at that. Of course, they shut it down and I had to start all over.

When American Tobacco closed and moved I had an opportunity to go with the company, but it would almost have been like starting over. It would have required moving to some little town down in North Carolina. But the long and the short of it was, I had children here. I had settled here. I'd lived here all my life. I didn't really want to leave the community, my children being in school, didn't want to disrupt family life any more than necessary. I could have gone to Philip Morris. Brown and Williamson might not have wanted me back, but I could have went to Philip Morris. I was an experienced operator, experienced in maintenance, so I had the qualifications that would have been required to get a job at one of those other two places. Lorillard was another. I thought, "It don't look good for the future. I'm going to opt into some other business line, something that's more secure." My loyalty to a particular company was immense and unending and had that place stayed in business, I'd probably still be there. I always did give everything my very best shot.

At the end of December of 1970 it was apparent that my job at American Tobacco would be ending within a month. Having been a radio operator for some time, I was in communication with a number of people around the area. A friend of mine advised me by way of our amateur radio system that a job opening was going to be available, it appeared, at Johnson Controls. He had changed his job and went there the previous fall, and one of the maintenance men there, an elderly gentleman, had suffered a heart attack. They hadn't replaced him and he wasn't doing too well at the time. January the 15th of '71 was my last day at American Tobacco. That job had forced me to bump down from a line maintenance mechanic to loading box cars on the loading dock, and my employment terminated there on the 15th of January. By about the 20th of January my friend Earl Goldsmith from over in Louisville urged me to come out and apply for a job there as much as they obviously needed a replacement. So I pursued that, went out, was interviewed by the gentleman at the plant who was in charge of maintenance and plant engineering, etcetera. He hired me and I went to work the following day, if I remember.

I was unemployed for a matter of about two weeks. I was prepared to wait until summer. With my severance pay, my profit sharing, my money I had put away, I was prepared to be a little bit more selective. Try to find something I could make a career of. After having considered the product that we made there at Johnson Controls, I figured, "Well, cars will never be out of business. As long as there's cars, they'll need batteries, looks like a pretty secure situation."

Well, the fact of the matter is, they were behind in their work. I got a job there, passed my physical and reported back. They were behind and it was like ten- and twelve-hour days. I think it must have been more than a month before I got a day off. I had a new job to learn, lots of new things to learn. All this equipment was entirely different from anything I'd worked on. I was busy doing that and paid little attention to the time. The money was good. I went to work there substantially at a higher wage than what I had been receiving. When I went to work there, I think the wage was like probably $3.75 an hour, and I had been making like $2.25 or something. It was a significant increase. I think we had better health insurance at Johnson Controls than I had been accustomed to. I liked the work. Always did enjoy a challenge and it was challenging. So I got a job there and advanced myself rather quickly and promised them nothing that I couldn't deliver.

Howard Etherton, International Harvester

My dad drove rock trucks and farmed. I don't guess daddy ever worked for anybody prior to going to work at Harvester in 1947 other than himself or driving a truck for somebody. The plant started there in 1946. There was a few people hired in '46 and then they done most of the hiring in '47 and '48. My dad was one of the older people, seniority people, there. Back in them days, they'd hire just anybody because there wasn't that many people to work. So anybody who wanted to go to work at Harvester back when dad went there just went in there and went to work. Back in the '40s when the old Harvester plant started, the old FE [Farm Equipment Workers Union Local 236] was in there and they was on strikes all the time. Then in 1955 they got out of the FE and brought the UAW [United Auto Workers] into the Harvester plant and they started getting good benefits then like insurance and holidays and so forth. I guess insurance is one thing that kept dad there until he retired, until he passed away.

I worked at GE doing construction work before I went in the Army. I went and registered and told them I was eighteen years old and got a registration card and then went over there and went to work at GE construction work when I was probably, I guess I was only fifteen, no more than sixteen. Then I got a notice in the mail to come to be examined for the Army and my mother threw a fit. She found out what I done. They stopped me from going then but then when I turned seventeen I joined. When I got out of the Army, I went to work at Pepsi-Cola for just a couple, three months until I could find something different. Then I went to work at GE probably in about September of '56, and then Harvester started hiring in February of '57 and my brother and I both went over there and went to work at Harvester.

I didn't like the work at GE as much as I thought I would at Harvester. I guess because my dad worked at Harvester and at that time at Harvester plants you made quite a bit more money than you did at GE. I just thought I would be better satisfied building tractors than I would refrigerators. So my brother and I both went to work there the same day. I figured I'd probably work there until I retired. When I started there they was looking at thirty years' retirement, and I figured I'd stay there thirty years and retire.

Danny Mann, Johnson Controls

When I was in high school I wanted to ride professional rodeo. I used to break horses and ride them bulls and that's what I wanted to do. Trubador had a mechanical bull and I loved that thing. The name of that bull was El Toro. My dad used to call me and Dennis, my best friend, El Dumbo for riding El Toro. It went from one to ten and most of them would ride it on four and they would get throwed. They tried it seven, shoo, they're off there. Well, when I got ready to ride they knew and they turned sirens on and all that because I was going to ride it on ten. I bit the fire out of that thing. I said, "I'm going to buy one of these things." But, you know, my dad talked me out of that one. I used to break horses up in Indiana and most of the time I did it for kicks, I didn't really charge. I guess it was that they can't and I can.

I worked at Kroger part-time during high school and was going to stay at Kroger. I had everything to go full-time and my manager canned me from going full-time because he wouldn't let me go to the warehouse. That's where the money was to be made, was at the warehouse. He rejected my bid to go. He wouldn't let me leave the store, because I was a good worker. I would have stayed with Kroger but I wanted to make more money. I think at that time you had to have like twelve weeks of forty hours. Well, they would run me eleven weeks at forty hours and drop me back to thirty hours so I couldn't get full-time. So it was like, well, gotta leave here.

Dad wanted me to be happy. He was very supportive. I started out at JCC [Jefferson Community College]. I thought I'm going to try JCC to see if I'm going to cut it. Well, when I went to JCC I went there for two semesters and I did okay. I was working and I had my mind on partying. Then I had a chance to go to Ford Motor Company so I said, "I'm not going to school." I've been very fortunate and I've had high-paying jobs. I lived at home 'til I was twenty-five because I had it made. I was very appreciative of my parents. Come Christmas time I didn't think nothing about spending a thousand dollars on each of them. While I was working at Ford I was living at home and all that and I would sock over half my check in the bank every week and that was in savings. The rest of it was to blow, but this was savings. I said, "Before I'm twenty-five I'll own half my own home." Everybody just laughed but I said, "I'm telling you." But I worked on it. I've always been a hard worker. During the week I don't duff it off, I'm there every day and I work. That's the way my father was, that's what he instilled in us. You go in there and give a guy a day's work for a day's pay. You don't go in there and goof off. I guess that kind of stuck.

I thought Ford was going to be there forever. I was at Ford probably two-and-a-half years. Then, see, they discontinued the LTD [model] and so they had that big layoff and I had made a bad choice of careers. A friend of mine, he told me, "Go put in an application, they [Johnson Controls] might be hiring some." I walked in there, put the application in. They read my resume which was handwritten and they said, "Can you start today?" By the time Ford called me back I had as much time in at Johnson Controls that I had at Ford. So I made a bad mistake and stayed with Johnson Controls, because the money was good and I liked the people. I felt like that place was going to be there forever, because I felt like everybody needed a battery. The money was good at Ford, the money was good at Johnson Controls but everybody's going to need a battery and that plant had been there for thirty years. Well, over thirty years. So I thought, well, "This plant's going to be here forever."

Johnson Controls gave a little lesser pay but you're on piece work, so the harder you work, the more you make. I was working with three guys who were good, hard workers and we made good money. And we produced a product, you know. The only way you got paid was by producing a product because you're on piece work. You made good money if you was on a good crew. Plus, you had to use your head more at Johnson Controls than you had to use your head at Ford. Because you didn't work on a line, you were a machine operator. Three sections of the plant you were machine operators, so you were using complex equipment and had to be able to set it up yourself. It was all based on piece work and you had designated times to change the machine over. Well, if you beat that rate and you got running then you made more money. There was a lot of heavier work at Johnson Controls. Everything in that plant was heavy. When you're dealing with lead and all that, every job in there was heavy.

I expected to retire. I didn't expect anything. Johnson Controls was a—let me put this politely—was a sneaky conglomeration of wannabees. You know, everybody, all the top management, management, not at the plant, not at our level, at corporate level, they were cutting throats right and left. There was no loyalty in corporations at all. I knew that, but you would expect a little bit of, you know, kindness or understanding.

I work with my hands for a living. I'm a blue-collar worker and I'm proud of being that. If it wasn't for blue collar this country wouldn't be what it is.

Rob McQueen, International Harvester

My father was a truck driver for a while. My mother was a waitress. My father was in the military and then when he got out he started right then as an over-the-road truck driver. He had a bad heart, had rheumatic fever when he was young. After he died mom got another job. Another waitress job. She worked two jobs as long as I can remember. Really it seemed like it was pretty much always like that. So I wanted to be a truck driver too. There's a picture somewhere of Dad putting me in his truck, and that was at that time all I wanted to be.

Of course, it changes. I went to high school and I had visions of playing basketball. Jobs were so easy back then. You didn't have to have a high school education. You didn't have to have much intelligence at all. You could walk out and Philip Morris, Harvester, railroad—you could get a job anywhere. Like at Harvester, it was something like this: I applied for the job, they called me the next day to have an interview the next day, and then a physical the next day, or possibly the same day, and then asked me right after the physical if I could start to work right then. It was pretty much everywhere at that point in time. I guess that's why there was quite a few dropouts back then because you was going to jobs that paid good money. At that point in time, I guess, being a South End boy, I never envisioned myself as working in an office. That wasn't for me anyway so there wasn't a lot of encouragement to finish high school and go on to college. Hell, you could just start right then and make good money. I think I said before I was making back at Harvester something like $12–13 an hour or something like that, and right now I'm not even at $10 an hour. And this was twenty years ago.

It really started because I got married. I had a girlfriend, she got pregnant. So I tried to work at Louisville Ladder and go to school, too, plus play basketball. Just couldn't do it. I wound up going to Ralston-Purina for a couple years. I had to have a good job cause by this time, my daughter was born. I was married and we bought a home in Valley Station. I thought, I need to get something better. So many places was hiring, like I said earlier, and I just happened to choose International Harvester. I thought, "They're making tractors and trucks and grass-cutting equipment and farming equipment," you know, "That'll be there forever." At that point in time, I was thinking they could lose railroads a lot easier than they'd want to do something with International Harvester. Dumb choice. But at the time, I thought I was making the right choice. I knew the pay was good and the benefits were good. I was thinking that of all places, Harvester was so established. I thought this would be the ideal place to work. This would be the ideal place to start out, get in, and be retired. It was twenty-five and out.

I was tickled to death when I first got the job. I went there and put in an application on a Tuesday. They asked me to come back Wednesday for a physical. So the next day I went for the physical, and they asked me if I could start to work right then and there. I said, "Well, I didn't bring nothing to eat. I don't really have work clothes and stuff." They said, "Well, can you start tomorrow? What shift do you want?" This was in the foundry. So I was just tickled to death. I was really happy to get the job. But, there was fifteen of us that was hired together. Walking over to get our safety shoes and glasses—we had to walk through the foundry to the storeroom—out of the fifteen, I think eleven of us arrived at the storeroom to get our safety shoes and glasses. The other four quit on the way walking over. It was that hot, dirty. I'll never forget it. It was a sight like I'd never seen. Iron being poured and sparks going everywhere. Course the thought went through my mind, "Robbie, do you really want to do this?" Of course, like I said, I needed that job and I needed the job bad. The money was good, so I went with it.

That first day it was probably the scaredest...is there such a word as "scaredest"? Oh, I was scared to death. I'd never done anything like that. The heat, the sand—the air was just full of smoke, ashes. I was really leery of it, but I guess it was the way I was raised.

I had made—oh, I don't want to call it a mistake because now I have a beautiful daughter, and she's given me a beautiful grandson. So I don't mean that as a mistake. At that point in time, I guess it might have been a mistake because I felt like I could have done something in basketball. I was a pretty decent athlete at that time. I had to have a job though. My family meant everything in the world to me. I hadn't yet had my son, at this point in time, but I had just bought a new home out in Valley Station under a FHA 235 loan. I said, "Well, this is what a man does." I might have to work a little harder than my brother at Philip Morris, and I might get a lot dirtier than him. But, at that point in time, I was making better money, better benefits so it was all worth it...I suppose.

Phil Nalley, International Harvester

My father is from Holy Cross, Kentucky and my mother's from Loretta. Growing up, there wasn't much work out in that area. The war came along and dad went off to do his stint. When he came back they were living with his mother and a couple of little kids and so they decided it was time to move to a city. Louisville was the biggest city that had the most production. Dad worked in construction at that time, so he wanted to come here to find a job and raise his family. The company he went to work for, which was Tube Turns, had quite a few government contracts, manufacturing pressure vessels and fittings. It was just natural coming from the military to look for that type of company, knowing that the military was always going to buy and it would always be a strong place to work. So that's basically what brought him here, employment opportunities.

He raised eleven children so he needed something that was secure, something that paid. Tube Turns had something called piece work, where the more work you did, the more money you made. So there was more opportunity for him to have a better income than a flat salary. He worked the same job for twenty-one years. He stayed on that job because, first of all, he had gained a lot of respect from the people there. They could depend on him to do a good job. They could depend on him to get the work out and it'd be done right. They treated him with a respect because of that. I know he felt good that he was accomplishing more than just a job. He was proud of what he did.

Dad encouraged vocational training and I went to DeSales High School, a Catholic high school. They really were a lot better back in the '70s in comparison to some of your public schools. They basically taught that you followed your father's footsteps. Dad—he was a firm believer in manual labor, working with your hands. He really did not like office people all that much. I'm not sure exactly why he had such a conflict with them, but he did. So I took vocational training as a welder during my junior and senior year of high school. Upon coming out I welded for several years and I thought about going back to school, which I talked to my dad about. He didn't think it was a good idea because I was going to quit my job and go back to Firestone or Kroger's, just one of the local businesses, for an income and try U of L [University of Louisville] for a while. He wasn't in favor of that and was very, very adamant about me continuing on with what I was doing. I was making decent money and I was good at what I did, but I thought possibly I wanted to try it, at least try something else. But it ended up like it has, which is okay. Coming from the South End, blue-collar working-class people, most didn't attend college and most fathers were in some type of manufacturing or labor position and so it's kind of following your father's footsteps, going that route.

In 1973 I was working at a company called the Marley Company. I took welding in a vocational school and I was practicing that trade. It went through a fluctuation of the market, and there were times that they would have layoffs. I think I was laid off a couple of times just for short periods of time. At that time you would roll into a lesser qualified job. They considered welding a skilled trade so you would go back into production. International Harvester was hiring, which paid about a dollar more on the hour than I was presently making plus it was one of the premier manufacturing companies here in the city to work at; that, Ford Motor Company, G.E., I guess was third and a few others. Other people were leaving the Marley Company, going out there and filling out applications and being hired, friends of mine that I went to school with that I would see out on Friday night or whatever. They hired you on the spot. They actually got to a point that they took people off the street that had never welded before and gave them three days of classes and taught them.

The automobile industry—Ford Motor Company—all you ever heard, and I knew people that worked there, was the assembly line work, how mundane it was and how it was so boring. They paid good, but they also worked quite a bit of overtime. And it was mandatory, there wasn't any choice. I didn't want to go into that type of setting. I wanted something that I felt was more interesting. I guess the lack of knowledge of International Harvester was probably one of the reasons also I went there, not knowing what I was going into. I could have gone to Ford Motor Company any time and filled out an application, but I didn't want to. G.E., they were going on strike all the time, that's all you ever heard on the news. They made washing machines and refrigerators and there again, another assembly line job. The [Harvester] foundry was not assembly line.

It was very eye-opening when you walked in. All the heat, the noise, at times was just deafening. You see in the movies how the sparks blow, that's real in the foundry. They lead you down through there on the first day, this iron zone is what they called it. There'd be forklifts coming down through there and they would have a ladle on the front of it that weighed several tons of molted iron and it would move within this ladle and it would splash out sometimes and when it hit the floor it would just explode into sparks and looked like a firework had gone off or something. It was April 3, it was fairly warm. Just going into this strange world, some of them felt they didn't need a job like that. They didn't need a job that bad. There again, in '73 you could go to a lot of places and get jobs. It wasn't like they were the only company here hiring.

I didn't quit because I was married. I had a son. I'd worked in a factory before. I was used to some noise. Welding is hot, there's a lot of sparks, you get burned quite often. I wasn't really seeing anything there that really looked out of line. I'd worked around presses that made a lot of noise that bent metal, I had worked around glue machines and just all kinds of rollers, conveyor belts; so I've seen a lot of things there that were familiar already. I don't believe in quitting right away. I may realize that it's not worth pursuing at a point but I have to at least try first and see what it's like.

Ron Phillips, Johnson Controls

I guess I just wanted something financially stable. We knew as soon as we got out of high school if we didn't go into college, we'd be getting drafted, which is what happened to me. I guess being middle class, that's what everybody did. They got out of school, they graduated, and they went to work. I guess just something like I did.

As soon as I graduated—I had sort of a scholarship, because I played football, to Western Kentucky [University]. I was going down for spring training. During that time, I got my draft notice. In other words, my deferment hadn't been put through yet and if it hadn't been put through, too late, too bad. I think I had two weeks to report down for that so I just went ahead and joined the Navy during that time span. If you joined, you had more of a choice what you wanted to do.

In the Army, they said, "Well you get your training order, you know where you're going." Back then it was Vietnam. We did one tour over there and that's enough. You've seen enough. I didn't really think about making the Navy my career. Even though the war did end three or four years later, '75, as soon as my time was up, I was getting out. I didn't do nothing for about three or four months. Just more or less adjust back to civilian life. Then, I guess it was time to start looking for work. A friend of mine, he had worked at Johnson Controls, and he just wanted to know if I wanted a job there. So that's how it came about.

Back then if you knew somebody that needed a job or wanted to work, you could more or less get these people in. It wasn't like it is now with all the tests and all the interviews and all that. You didn't have none of that. I just walked in and they said, "You start to work tomorrow morning." I think I filled out an application about a month after I started there. That's how a lot of people did back then. A lot of people go to work a few days, they quit. So it's just a waste of time to do that. The economy was booming. I guess usually in wartime it is. I could have went to Ford but this place here was paying maybe a quarter more an hour. I think my starting pay was $3.51 an hour, and that was in '71. It don't sound like much now but I guess back then it was. Plus, hospitalization, medical, pension, life insurance. I didn't have to pay nothing. Dental, eye glasses. It was all furnished.

Bob Reed, Johnson Controls

My father was in the tire business. He was a traveling salesman. He was a commercial artist. He drew landscaping pictures for people and for construction companies. They'd go in there and they would construct buildings over what he drew up. He delved into all kinds of different types of things and he wasn't really restricted. I don't understand why he got into the tire business because I couldn't stand it myself. My brother and I worked with him for a while. I think basically all he wanted to do was be a salesman. He could sell anybody anything. He even worked for Paramount Studios out in California. I don't even know what he did out there. We heard a lot of stories that he worked for all the professional actors. He did everything, he wasn't limited to one particular thing.

So, I wanted a structured life. We moved all the time. I don't know how many times when we were kids. We went to about ten or fifteen different grade schools in the eight years that I went to grade schools. We went even to Miami, Florida; Owensboro, Kentucky;

went to about six or seven here in the city of Louisville and we were all over the place. When I was a freshman in high school I said I know exactly what I want to do. I want to settle down. I'm not going to run off and do all these other kinds of jobs, I want to stick in one particular field. I've got a little bit of art ability, that's what I want to pursue. Of course, it didn't turn out the way I wanted it to. A lot of things don't ever turn out the way you want. But, I knew that's not what I wanted. You've got to have one thing you pursue and stick with it. That way you might be able to excel in that area.

I had so many expectations, so many dreams. I was going to start out when I graduated, start out as a freshman in college in art. I met a girl as a senior in high school and she was going to college in Florida that was strictly art oriented, and I really wanted to do that. But my dad died during my senior year and I said, "Well, I'm going to stay at home, I got to support mom and the family, try to get things squared away." I said, "Well, I know what I have to do." So once I started working it changed everything. I was out there working eight hours a day doing different things and I said, "This is what I have to do for a while." Then I got into the factory work at Johnson Controls, started making pretty good money after a while, and had good benefits and I was stuck in that mold of being a factory worker.

Geez, I wish I could have changed it, I really do. I wanted to go to school. There was a lot of things I didn't want to do that my parents did when I was growing up. I wanted a house and I wanted to pay for it. I didn't want to move like we did when we were kids, constantly moving all the time going from here to there. I want my yard. I want a nice house, a car, and all that. But I don't want to live in a mansion. I'm being realistic, I don't want the moon.

My first job out of high school was I worked at Nash Distillers in the office for about six months I guess. I was eligible for the draft at the time. They drafted a buddy of mine and his lottery number was right below mine. I figured I was next, I figured I was going to be drafted and I was going into the Army, go either to Vietnam or whatever. So I told the people there, I said, "I've got to leave, I cannot stay here because I've got to pursue a couple of other things I need to do." So I quit. Thank God they didn't draft me. . . . But, I had missed a good opportunity.

I didn't really like working there. I didn't really like working in an office. To me that's not me. I want to work with my hands. It's either the art ability or pursuing other interests, but sitting down at a desk doing that type of work never interested me. I've got to be creative, I've got to do something. But sitting at a desk, doing numbers, you know, filling out reports and that stuff is not me.

So then I started working for a clothing warehouse, Webster Sportswear. They gave me the opportunity to take over the raincoat warehouse. They had certain sections of the warehouse where people took charge. They put me in charge of this whole big area and it was a mess. It was totally chaotic, so I went down there and straightened it all out, put a board up there and gave them directions so somebody could come down there and go to a certain area and pick what they wanted and it was all straightened out. It was okay but the pay was the worst part of it. They didn't want to pay you anything so that was kind of disheartening. So, I said it's about time. I wanted more money.

My first wife, a friend of hers worked at Johnson Controls at the time and so he recommended me to go in and talk to the general foreman at the time. I went in and talked to him and got the job the next day. That was 1972, May of 1972. I started within two or three days. I was hired right on the spot when I talked to him. I had a better chance to better myself than working in a warehouse because it pretty well limits you as to what you can do. Although I had a lot of responsibility at the warehouse, I figured working in a production and a manufacturing company might give me more opportunity to make more money and I might get a supervision job, something like that.

Kenny Rhodes, International Harvester

My father worked for an outfit called Curtiss-Wright, which was in the old International Harvester building, and he was a buyer. He was buying parts, machines, like the big green doors that you used to lift up and down on the side of the buildings. I think it got on his nerves real bad and his doctor told him if he didn't find him another line of work he was going to have a heart attack. So my dad said, "Well, what do you suggest?" And he said, "Why don't you go drive a truck?" So he went down and got a truck-driving job and started driving a truck. That's how he started and he did it the rest of his life. I probably resented it because I was very sports oriented; I played a lot of football and stuff such as that, and I'd like for him to be able to come to the games. He couldn't because he was gone all the time. But he did make us a good living and we had a good life so I guess it's a trade-off. It's probably no different than businessmen traveling all over the country or world or whatever. He was home when he could be there and it was pretty quality time when he was there. So it was livable.

I thought I'd play football, more than likely. That's the best I remember because I didn't really have any desire to be a doctor or dentist or anything like that. I did think in high school that I might be a lawyer, but I got married young and had my daughter and that was that. I basically come from a blue-collar family. My dad drove a truck and I guess that's about pretty much what I was in line to do. I was either going to go there or Ford Motor Company or somewhere like that. Primarily factory work. Of course, in the '60s it was easier to get a factory job than it is now. My first job, I started as a paper boy. I believe I was about thirteen. After that I went to work at a filling station, it was an ESSO. I worked there while I was in school and I stayed there 'til I was almost eighteen years old. And then I went to International Harvester.

My brother Tommy worked there. They were hiring and some friends of our family knew the president of that local, Carl Richman, and they talked to him and Carl talked to Bob Sands, which was the industrial manager or personnel manager, and they let me come in. They were just basically hiring anybody who come through the door. There was a lot of jobs and not a lot of people at the time, plus the war was still going on so that made it easier to get in. I could have went to Ford or Harvester or GE or whatever and I just took Harvester. I thought working around tractors and stuff would be more interesting than building cars. Plus, it was the first one to come available and I knew I was going to have a child and I needed a job, so I went with it.

I was pretty excited about it. There was fifty people that were in that day and I was the last one in the room to be called. But I [by chance] was the first one [to get] in line to [pick up] the clock card number, which made me senior over all the other forty-nine. That worked out real well for me. You get down to being laid off, it makes all the difference in the world. If they lay off thirty people you stay, they go.

The first day wasn't too awful bad but the second day was when it got bad. The first day was just going through the fundamentals: the physical; filling out the applications, insurance, and all that sort of stuff; introducing you to the place and showing you who your boss was going to be and kind of walking you around and telling you what was expected. Then they sent us home. Then the next day we had to be there at seven o'clock and that's when it got interesting.

I planned on being there 'til I retired. Well, I just figured it was a good place to work and they had a decent pension for back then, and I just figured I was going to be there. I never really even thought much about anything else. I started out, it seems like I was $3.27 an hour when I started but that was 1968. That wasn't bad. Plus, you know, you had time and a half, double time, all that for your over time. So you could make a living. That was decent money. It went a lot further back then. I just felt like [factory work] was probably the best I could do at the time because at the time I didn't have a high school diploma and I felt pretty lucky to even be able to have gotten a job like that.

Marilyn Reed, Johnson Controls

My dad was a salesman. He worked in a clothing store. He was an insurance salesman. And, he was a baker. He was a baker most of my life. We had a bakery and we used to work in it, my brother and I. When I was thirteen, I guess. We'd glaze doughnuts, help with the Danish, and things like that, and work out front at the counter. I had thought I would have liked to have been a physical education teacher, but I didn't really go about it or anything. I just kind of went along with the flow and did what everybody else was doing. I think not a lot went to college back then. Most everybody got married when they was in their twenties. I got married when I was nineteen. My dad always said, "Well, you need to be a secretary," he said, "because that's what most girls do." And he said, "You don't need to go to college because you'll get married." That's what I did. I was a secretary after I got out of school.

My first job out of school was customer service clerk. I typed up purchase orders, and proofread them and things like that, at the Louisville Chair Company. I worked there about a year. Then I got pregnant with my son, and my husband didn't want me to work. Then I got pregnant with my daughter when my son was six months old. So, he still didn't want me to work. But I wanted to work, and we needed extra income because he wasn't making enough money. So, I went to work at Kentucky Packaging Company—they sold corrugated cardboard—and I worked in the office there. I answered the phone and things like that. I worked there for three months. Then he joined the service and we moved out to California. Then he went to Vietnam, and he was there for a year. He came back, and he stayed in the service and didn't know what he was going to do. He had a tour in Japan, and so I was in Japan for fifteen months. I left him over there and came home with my children, and divorced him. Then I got a job at Johnson Controls.

My husband's sister got me the job. She said there was an opening so if I wanted to come over and interview. So she set that up. I just remember going in there and Jim Hudson was the personnel manager and I talked to him and I guess it was pretty much she got me the job because she told him I was coming. They hired me, just lickety-split.

Mike Reid, Johnson Controls

My dad was a plumber. Self-employed. He made a lot of money. He worked a lot of hours, fourteen, fifteen hours a day, every day. Except Sundays. He wouldn't work but about a half a day Sunday. His brother was a plumber. He worked at Ford, G.E., did those factory things and then he was working with his brother on the side and then he just decided to stay in plumbing. He had gotten laid off at Ford and just went straight from there to plumbing.

So, I was working with him on a Saturday and it was pouring down rain, I remember it well. We were working for this lady who was personnel manager at Johnson Controls and she came down there and asked me if I'd like to have a job making sixteen to eighteen dollars an hour and I said, "Sure." It was closer to fifteen and that was April of '79. That was big bucks back then, still is. I think she came up with it on the spot when she saw me standing out in the rain digging a ditch. She was impressed. Pretty much when I went in there, filled out the application, and handed it to her she said, "Go get a physical." When I got back from the physical she said, "Go to work." I started on second shift. I did all this stuff in the morning and then started at 2:30 in the afternoon on second shift. I was rolling in the dough. I had hit the big one.

Frank Reinhart, Johnson Controls

I was going to get into being a federal agent. But that went downhill. I gave that up. I went to a vocational school and all that and I was working part-time at the police station and worked there two years and was about ready to go into the service and things just kind of changed then. I had it all mapped out but never did go through. I got married when I was fifteen and then I was divorced at about seventeen and a half. When I got married at fifteen, I quit right at my sophomore year and then I went into a vocational program, National Youth Corp, got my GED there. You went to school half a day and then you went on to the job training and they paid you to go to school and stuff.

Then I worked at a uniform place where I would go to Indianapolis, Cincinnati, and Danville five days a week and drop off stuff. I think I was there about three years. I drove a delivery truck, dropping off pop, like selling them to the stores. It was all right but I quit there because they had me on this one route and there was two times I got robbed and one time I got beat up and I told them, you know, tell the store manager or whatever, I think it was at a liquor store, that nobody was going to make his deliveries unless he controlled the situation around the store. So they wouldn't do it so I just told them that I quit.

Back then you could quit one job and go to another one. Just go down to the state employment office and they would have like, say for instance, they would hire for Ford, hire for Louisville Slugger. They'd send you out some things and at the time I had an interview for Ford, I interviewed for Johnson Controls. I had some friends who worked out at Ford and they told me Johnson Controls was just as good money as Ford, you worked harder at Ford and they broke you down, at the time. That was basically why I chose them. I didn't know nothing about all of the toxic stuff you'd be working around though, the lead and stuff like that. The good thing of it was, Ford would only last about five years compared to almost eighteen at Johnson Controls. Those friends of mine, they was laid off and they never was called back.

Thomas Rhodes, International Harvester

My dad drove a truck and made pretty good money. He was an owner/operator. He was a teamster—it was a union job—but dad was making $40,000 to $45,000 a year thirty years ago. He lived in that truck. If the wheels ain't turning, you ain't making any money. It's just that simple. He was very conscientious about it. I know there was a lot of our old neighbors that always wondered how this damn truck driver lived as good or better than they did. But he was gone for a week or two at a time and they was home every night. That's how.

Well, to be honest with you I didn't know what I was going to do. It was never really something that I thought too much about. School was something that I didn't particularly like. I didn't do badly but I never really did great. Looking back I'm sure I could have done much better than I did, but it wasn't what my interests were in. I was interested in fooling around with my car and chasing girls. That's as honest as can be.

I went through high school. I went to work before I graduated. I worked part-time at what they called Distributive Education back then. You go to school half a day and they release you to go to a job and work for half a day. In fact, I worked for my stepfather at a service station. I worked for him for a couple, three years. I had worked part-time on the weekends and some after school for another fellow just up the street, but just strictly on a part-time, after school and weekends, that type of thing. I had carried newspapers prior to that. When I graduated high school I was married and had a son. We got married when I was seventeen, and so when I left high school I knew what I needed was a job, and I went to get a job. That's about as straight and simple as it gets. I mean, that's the only thing that was on my mind.

Well, it was just luck, it was just a thing that happened. I used to work part-time at a Phillips 66 station. The guy that run it, Frank Boyd, his son and I were close friends; his name was Richard. I stopped in there one morning to get gas on the way to Ford. My dad had set up an appointment for me to go over there and get a job. My dad was a truck driver but he was close friends with the plant manager over there. But anyway, I stopped to get gas and Richard and a couple of his buddies, they were in there and they were getting ready to go to Harvester. Harvester was hiring. Back then there were all kinds of jobs. It was just a matter of going and telling them, "I want a job." Seriously, it really was. He said, "Well, come on and go with us." I thought, "What the heck." So we all went to Harvester and we all got hired. So that's really how I went to Harvester instead of Ford. I was eighteen years old. I went to work at Harvester on the 7th of January in '65. That was four days after my eighteenth birthday—my birthday is January 3rd. The only thing that I really knew about them was that it was a good paying job, they had good benefits.

At that time, literally there were a lot of jobs. You could have went to any one of many companies in the town, several of which no longer exist, and gotten jobs. There were a lot of jobs available. Some better than others but there were any number of places. I mean, it was just a matter of going and walking in and saying, "Here I am." Basically. I mean, you had a job. GE, Ford Motor Company, Brown and Williamson—which no longer is here—Phillip Morris, the Marley Company, American Air Filter. They used to have weight restrictions but I can't remember what they were. At least minimum restrictions, I think like 125 pounds or something like that. A high school diploma wasn't necessary; pass a physical, which was really about like going into the Army which is a joke. If you can walk and balance a fork cock-eyed then you're good. Just basic pretty simple things. Nothing of any serious consequence other than you had to be eighteen. They wanted you to be big enough and strong enough because there was a lot of heavy lifting and heavy jobs and things to do. But things were booming and everybody was hiring people. Jobs were plentiful, there were plenty of jobs in this town.

CHAPTER 2

"The Dangers of Some of the Jobs Was Unreal"

"Can you tell me about your job?" In response to this general and on the surface simple question, the former employees of International Harvester and Johnson Controls launched into detailed, vivid accounts of the tasks involved in producing iron machine parts and automotive batteries. Their answers to this question demonstrated a contradiction in assumptions and imperatives; the narrators assumed a familiarity with the nature of heavy industry on the part of the interviewers and did not stop to give the full name of equipment or job titles or to explain a step in a process. But at the same time, the urgency of their tone and repetition of particular images revealed a need to make the interviewer, an outsider to industrial work, grasp the severity of the conditions under which they worked. Indeed, the primary theme that arose from this section of the narratives was the health and safety challenges in both plants, detailed accounts of which are woven through every aspect of the description of the jobs there. The narrators insist, explicitly at times but also by suggestion, that the physically demanding nature of their jobs required a high level of skill that only a certain kind of person—intelligent, resourceful, and with a strong work ethic—could succeed in these conditions and, foreshadowing later arguments, that these traits ought to have been, but were not always, recognized by management.

In this chapter narrators explain the tasks involved with their jobs and comment on their skill and performance in completing them; paint a graphic picture of the dangers they faced on a daily basis and some of the precautions the company was forced to take or that employees themselves devised to survive them; and pass judgment on the job and the companies. The chapter is organized into three sections focusing on each of these themes. Within each section there are narratives about International Harvester first, followed by those about Johnson Controls. We have grouped the narratives by workplace in order to facilitate understanding of the different work processes. We have chosen to replicate the narrators' habit of assuming basic knowledge about industrial workplaces—using only their language and not adding explanation for how the plant operated—with the hope of facilitating the reader's immersion in the story and in the perspective of the people who were in the plant every day. Put another way, the goal of this chapter is to allow the former employees of International Harvester and Johnson Controls to put the reader into their world through their words.

In this first section, workers from International Harvester describe the jobs they had and the tasks involved.

Phil Nalley, International Harvester

The first job I had, it was a lot more difficult than what I left. Just the first day running the machine because there was a lot of things you had to learn quickly. You had to work in this heat. You had to wear heavy clothes to keep the heat off of you. There was a lot of gases that were produced from the sand that had a mix of chemicals. As it baked it got hard and this chemical would produce a very ammonia type smelling gas and it would burn your eyes, irritate your throat, your nose. Approximately fifty percent of the people that hired in with me the first day quit. That in itself was somewhat disturbing thinking, well, "Can I do this? A lot of other people that are bigger or look to be stronger or maybe smarter and they can't do it so what makes me think that I can?" But that may be just my upbringing. In a family of eleven kids you learn to do a whole lot and withstand quite a bit.

When I got to the mill room as my permanent position they put me in an area called core knock-out. Cores that are made in the pour room, they went to the iron zone. That's where they poured all the castings and the castings rode on a belt for about three hours, or actually it was a conveyor. They finally got to the pour room and you would take these castings off that were encrusted with this black sand. You would lift them off the line and you would set them in a huge shaker and it would shake all this sand off. One person would set it up at the front of this shaker and put them in. And one person at the back would pick them up and rehang them on the line, so that it would send them on down to the mill room where they'd clean them up to be milled down to the finished product. It was May when I got up into that area—it was a normal, fairly warm month. I worked up there for about three months and the average temperature was somewhere around 212 degrees or above, we didn't really know. We had metal decking floors and you could spray water on them and the water would boil off the floor.

You worked thirty minutes and then you rested for thirty minutes. You'd work only four hours a day actually on the job and then they gave you that other four hours to try to recoup, replenish your water and your salts, and go back at it again. And, it was a very demanding job. Castings came out at somewhere about 1800 degrees, your larger ones. The smaller ones naturally were cooler, the heat would dissipate a lot quicker out of them. But we had some the size of your car out there and they called them a main frame. And those things at times, when the summer was really hot, you would bring them down the shaker and the iron would not be solidified yet and it would actually roll out of these things. Iron is twenty-three or so hundred degrees, is what it was melting at.

I also worked on what they called the trim lines. As these castings came down from core knock-out they rolled this conveyor for a period of time to cool down to a point where they would use a sand-blasting process to knock off all the remaining sand that was on these castings and then the casting was taken off and set on a conveyor belt. Then you would use a chisel—it was an air gun, you put the chisel in the air gun—and then you would trim off all the excess metals. That was probably one of the hardest jobs in the place. Not only did it take a lot of strength and stamina to do it, it was just so much vibration that you had to withstand in an eight-hour period. These belts would run one right after the next so as soon as you would finish one you would be going to the next one; there would not be a period where you would stop. You held in your left hand, if you were right-handed, a chisel that slipped up inside of this gun. The gun itself weighed about eight to ten pounds. As you pulled the trigger back it had a piston action that made the chisel go in and out and that's what cut this metal off. There were times you would cut off fairly big pieces and it would take some doing to get those cut off. Extremely noisy and very hot. The castings were still, depending on the size of them, most of them were hot enough still to burn you if you're working just in a T-shirt or something.

I did that type job. I couldn't tell you how many jobs I had over nine years. I did something called a mix coating for the cores that they made up in the core room. That was just like a mud bath that they would dip these things in, which would not allow the iron to penetrate this core. It was just like a sealer you're putting on it basically. This stuff came in a huge cardboard box and it looked just like red clay mud. There was a certain amount of the clay that you would add to water and you would have to measure and you would have to meet a certain consistency to be considered a correct mix. Too heavy, it would not coat the small holes or indentations in the core; it would not flow properly. And too light, it wouldn't coat it well enough to keep the iron from burning in. If you got a round, smooth cylinder as a core, when you took that out the inside of whatever you made was smooth and round. If that iron burned into that, now wherever it's burned, you would have a bump that would have to come out. So it was fairly interesting job—very, very dirty. I mean, I would be covered with this clay and I looked like I'd been a mud wrestler. All my clothes would just be totally covered with it. I would always take a couple of sets of clothing to change if it got real bad.

I was a painter there for awhile, as an absentee replacement. One of the guys that was a painter, he had emphysema and they put him off work and they just kind of gave me the job to do because I knew how to do it. Going to high school, going to a vocational school I played around in the auto repair department and played with the spray gun. I knew the basic set up. I didn't know exactly everything but once they saw I knew how to pull the trigger and mix the paint they said, "Oh yeah, he knows how to do it." So I did that for four or five months I guess it was. I was a forklift operator numerous times. I worked third shift clean-up crew. At the end of the day would clean these machines and have them spotless and ready to go for the next day's operation. I had jobs that are like babysitting the electric furnaces. All you did was sit in there and look at gauges and take readings so many times every hour and record all your temperatures and voltage use and amperage. If there was ever to be a problem it would always tell you right there on one of your gauges, which you have about thirty or so gauges that you watched continuously. If you had a problem in that area, you had a serious problem—a huge explosion. It really paid good because there was that element of danger. You'd better be there or if you weren't you were in big trouble. The company would not put up with people neglecting that particular job.

I had an attitude that whatever job I had I tried to do to the best of my ability because it paid me the most amount of money. I've got to be there for eight hours, I would just as soon make three more dollars on the hour as to make the least amount that I possibly can and still have to be there all day. I found by being busy, time passed. Doing mundane, repetitive type work, if you weren't busy, you were just constantly thinking about not wanting to be there, wanting to do something else. So, with that mindset I wanted to make the most money as I possibly could because I was there eight hours a day, five days a week. So why make the least amount I can if I still have to be there? But there were a lot of people there that they didn't care, they still made a good wage, it really didn't matter to them.

I aligned myself with supervisors that were known to take care of their people. There was a camaraderie and loyalty that would develop. There were seven of us that ran together for five or six years up there and we followed each other from department to department and we always tried to get to work for the same people and it was kind of like a crew that we developed. By all of us working together, we trusted each other and we would take care of each other. You knew the foremens out there that all they were there for was to come in and get their paycheck, as a lot of the employees were also. You stayed away from those if you could because they could care less. So the foremens that I worked for, in all the areas, I deliberately looked at those people and, yeah, that's who I want to work for; I see this individual taking care of his people. You might have three foremens in a particular department, they all do the same job basically but you've got one foreman who's taking really good care of his twenty. Well, why wouldn't you want to work for him? You know, you're all going to get paid the same but this guy here is willing to go to bat for you or willing to go the extra mile.

There were a lot of nights I would think, "Where did the time go?" Just actually by going through the same motions over and over again and practicing and trying to make it faster and trying to make it better and believing in a quality product, not just producing but actually making something that's good. If you're interested in staying busy, in keeping your job interesting, you can. A lot of these jobs, they were hopeless, and those were the ones that were really trying. The scale on these jobs were through the roof and you really couldn't make piecework on them. You knew that going into it but you still had to be there eight hours. So you make a decision, do you just let time drag or do you still try just to get through your day. So, I would be off at Rough River. I would be thinking about my kids growing up or whatever, just thinking about anything of interest. I would sneak a walkman in and put the speakers inside my earmuffs and listen to music which they didn't want us to do but I really didn't see the harm in it. I could understand some people not doing it because they didn't pay attention anyway, but if you paid attention to what you were doing—and I didn't want to get hurt. I've seen people lose hands and get burnt really bad and die so I knew there was a lot of danger there—I wanted to leave out of there every day like I came in pretty much.

Winfred Shake, International Harvester

I stayed in shipping for about fifteen years. Then I left and went to service parts. Then I went to the hospital area—that was tractor repair—and then from there I went to motor test, testing engines. Then from that I went to the engine assembly line. The last year of my employment there I worked in heat treat. They quit producing tractors there. Well, they was making those small lawn tractors and we quit making engines. So all that they were doing was machines and the small lawn tractors. Then they done the forging, but then they closed in '84. I went out in January of '82 [after] 34.7 years.

The main part of the job was loading tractors on flat cars for shipping, tying them down for shipping to the dealers. Service parts, I was the shipping clerk there. We shipped the parts out to different dealers and also some of the machine forges we shipped out to various plants.

[The hospital area] that was tractor repair. Tractors would come off the assembly line that had things wrong with them where either they had a noise in the engine or transmission or dented parts. We had to rework things. Up in engine test that's where the engines were tested after they was assembled. I was a tester up there and also a repairman. If they developed a knock then it was my job to see what the knock was, whether it was a loose rod or if the valve springs was set wrong or something. If the timing gears was noisy, change them. Then they'd be retested. Then out on the engine assembly line I worked from one end, from the finished engine to the starting of the engine, the bare block, I worked myself back through the positions.

[Heat treatment] was where the gears and various parts were heated to a certain temperature to case harden. They was put into a furnace and heated to a certain degree for so long a time. I had to load the racks and then empty the racks and send them on to various departments. I was what they called a furnace operator. As furnace operator I loaded and ran the parts through the heat treat, through the oven. Then after they was in so long a time then I had to unload the racks and put them on the proper racks and ship them to the various departments or send them to the various departments for further work or assembly.

Rob McQueen, International Harvester

I worked in every department, every shift, and I pretty much, believe this or not, could do just about every job. There was a bunch of them. I wasn't afraid of work and my foreman knew that. They knew that I was willing to do just about anything. I was a good machine operator. They wasn't afraid to send Mac, which was my nickname there, short for McQueen—they weren't afraid to send Mac over here to this machine and get him started on it cause they knew after a few minutes, I'd say, "Okay. I'm fine. I've got it."

This second set of narratives describe the tasks involved in the production of batteries at Johnson Controls.

Danny Mann, Johnson Controls

I always worked on the end of the plant that made the most money. I don't want to work on the end that's easier work, why should I make eleven dollars an hour when I can make sixteen or seventeen? We had one crew that I was on that all of us got together and man, we was like clockwork. I mean, we worked like a Swiss watch. We were on piecework. Three hundred batteries is a perfect night. That may be twelve hours pay in an eight-hour period. We run three hundred and we started at 2:30 and worked until 11:00. That's the time you got off. All right, and you had your break time and your shower times in there and stuff. We could be done at 9:30 because we wouldn't run on the cycle time. It was supposed to be on a thirty-four second cycle. But, as long as you keep your mote—you had a good COS [cast on strap machine operator] operating—if he'd keep his mote clean and his temperature down, you could rock. But you worked. So we asked the foreman, "If we give you three hundred batteries and we shut off early, are you going to tell upper management that we're shutting off early?" "Boys, if you give me three hundred batteries, I don't care if you shut off fifteen minutes after you start. As long as you don't get yourself in trouble you won't hear nothing from me." I said, "All right. Now this is, I'm getting your word, you know, nothing can be written; I've got your word, man to man?" "Yes." We'd give him three hundred like that. Because we would crank. We worked well together.

You had set jobs like your COS operator, what they called a loader and a stacker operator; we could all three run all the equipment. One guy would be back there throwing containers on a line. Robbie might run up there and he'd be loading my machine to keep it running; he'd run back up there and catch his up and I'd be over there doing Wayne's, catching Wayne back up. We was knocking them out. And the welder operator, who had more time than we did, who was in a different department, he was making the same money, or he was getting the same amount of batteries that we were getting, he'd come up there and we would rock and roll.

But, we were very young in seniority and they'd get laid off. Well, when we went back, they said, "Danny, would you take line five?" I said, "I'll take line five if you can get Wayne Lewis, if you can get Wayne Thompson and Robbie Gassinger. If you can swing it so that those guys end up being called back to that line," I said "I'll go." He said, "We can't do that." "Yes you can. If you use your head, you're management." "If you use your head, you can work this thing right and they can't touch you."' I said, "See, I'm dumb, I don't have no degree boys." I said, "I can figure out how to do it. If I can figure it, you can figure it." And, "I know we're going to end up in trouble over that one." "I'm telling you as a union rep I know these things; they can't touch you. If you figure it correctly." But it didn't pan out because Wayne quit and went to open his own business.

You had to use your head more at Johnson Controls than you had to use your head at Ford. Because you didn't work on a line, you were a machine operator. Three sections of the plant you were machine operators so you were using complex equipment and had to be able to set it up yourself. It was all based on piecework and you had designated times to change the machine over. Well, if you beat that rate and you got running, then you made more money.

I started there on what they called a reed stacker and I stayed with this because it was a good job. I had a good crew and until they had a cutback—I got laid off at Johnson Controls probably about three years in a row for about three months at a time. So then I went to a couple of other jobs in the plant but the reed stacker was where the money was at. That end of the plant was where the money was at. It was a lot harder work but that's where you made the most money. I could put up with just about anything if the money's right. I'd get laid off and they'd bring you back to another job in the plant, in the shipping department, over in the formation department, and then as soon as a bid come open to go back to fourteen, I was gone. A lot of guys tried it but they couldn't swing the machinery down there. You can just about tell all the way through the plant where people work, I mean, where they're going to work. Guys who had been there twenty-five years, they were not going to go to that end of the plant because the machinery, the set-up, and everything would just kill them, they couldn't do it. Running a reed stacker, you're probably lifting about two and a half to three tons a night. And the COS operator, he did the same, because everything you ran he had to pick up. You had two stacks of plates— well, if you're running an even group which is ten, eight, sixteen or odd plate then you had three trucks of plates and you'd pick the plates up and they were in stacks of fifty and they probably weighed between ten and fifteen pounds per stack. And there'd be like oh, I'd say, 120,000 per truck, your negatives 120,000, your positives 120,000. You rope those and you threw out all the bad plates that came out. You sort the plates and you ran them through the machine and there was a separator and later they went to an envelope that your plate went into—that your negative plate went into—to keep you from shorting out the battery. Then you put the group out and it ran through COS and then they put the straps on and then it's dropped into the container.

If you couldn't get your machinery to run right, if you had bad plates or sometimes the mud was falling out of the plates or whatever— you had to learn tricks to run them. You just had to learn little tricks to make the machine run. When they went to the backing system, trying to set the deck height and all that to make it pick one plate up and not two—you couldn't have two plates in the same envelope—to make it pick up one at the time was pretty tricky. We got to where we started sticking duct tape over the holes learning that that was a better way to do it because the machine wouldn't adjust down enough. So there's a lot of little tricks that we used to do.

Buddy Pugh, Johnson Controls

I worked on what they call the assembly line. I don't know what the title of my job was—just general laborer I guess. I did just about almost everything with the exception of a couple of jobs in the whole plant. Of course, I worked there nearly thirty-two years. I worked on what they called battery assembly. Out of the thirty-two years I worked in battery assembly for probably thirty years. It was machine operations.

Putting the battery cells together and putting them in the container, putting the top on the container. Putting the cell together consisted of battery plant plates, lead plates, lead oxide plates, and they were ran through one machine that made different size grooves. This consisted of worn element when they came out of the machine because a groove and an element was the same thing. I ran this machine for a long, long time. Then I went to what they called a COS machine which took bolted lead and united these element plates, these plates and these elements and put those in a container on the line. I did that for a number of years. My final job when I was there, I was what they call a utility operator which consisted of doing both of these jobs plus I did a welder job that united these elements together by welds, by electrical welds and putting tops on these batteries. I did all these jobs. That wasn't my regular job but that was a fill-in job that I did and that was just part of the utility job. The rest of it was set-up operators, trouble-shooter, and gopher or whatever. It consisted of a number of jobs. There were no really good jobs there. Believe me, there was no really good jobs there. But that's the job [utility] that I liked best.

Bob Reed, Johnson Controls

They knew who the good operators were. They could trust all of them to run good quality. I don't know how many times they would come back in the department and say, "Well, we want such and such's material, his production because we know his stuff is going to run real well." Come back and say, "Well, we want Bob Reed's production. We want so-and-so. We want Norman Horvach's production. We want this guy's production. These grids are good grids." And we'd always run good production. So they knew who was good and who was not. But these certain individuals that ran this stuff knew how to run it, were conscientious about their jobs.

Regardless of whether I liked that place, whether I liked Johnson Controls or I didn't, I knew I had a job to do. I did the best, I ran the best quality I could run and I was proud of what I did and I took pride in what I ran. I got compliments from other departments saying that I did good stuff and I guess about three or four other operators did too. But the majority of the people were greedy and they wanted to run what they could run and they didn't care about the quality and they had a lot of problems with their production. But four people can't run everything. Those foremen would come up to you and tell you, say, "Bob, we know you run good stuff." Or Joe or Jim or whatever. He said, "Keep up the good work," every so often . They wouldn't pat you on the back, "Good job," or nothing like that. It wasn't any kind of, I guess, incentive there. I guess you don't expect that in a plant like that, but sure goes a long way into making you feel like you're a valued employee or that you're doing a good job when you hear it.

In this narrative Charlie Noyes describes the particular issues that arose being a maintenance worker, rather than a machine operator or assembly-line employee, at the battery plant, and his attitude toward the job.

Charlie Noyes, Johnson Controls

I've been asked to do things I knew were beyond the scope of what was reasonable and I refused to do them. In one instance, a younger man who had come there from a catalyst plant, several employees came there from it. They came there, young and new and dumb. I was asked to crawl out on a board one time over an acid tank to repair a wire and I wouldn't do it. So my boss went and got one of these young guys and he did. The board broke and he fell into the acid tank. And that can be mean stuff, let me tell you. But it didn't produce any lasting injuries, thank God. There wasn't that much in there. But I knew better—just common sense told me that wasn't the thing to do. We all make our share of mistakes.

[In another incident] I had taken second shift, I think it was, for a period of two weeks. There was two guys that were on vacation and another boy, a younger fellow, had to do the same. There was two departments to cover and I chose one, which left the younger fellow with the other one.... The second shift maintenance foreman, who happened to be in charge of Saturday's work, got perturbed with this boy or myself, one or perhaps both of us and put us to clean a pit. It didn't bother me but it upset this youngster to some degree. I told him, "Look at it this way. You're still making the same money. You got the same number of hours to put in. If that's what this fellow wants us to do, let's show him we can do the very best job that he's ever had done." And so we did. We sat down and we cleaned that old dirty pit out. It was basically spotless when we got through. When the maintenance superintendent come in on Monday morning and wanted to know what we had done, we told him. He couldn't believe it. He went and looked, but he couldn't believe it. That other foreman got in a world of trouble. That was kind of a unique experience.

No matter what they give you to do just do the best you can possibly do. That's always been my attitude and probably always will be. I may not be able to do everything, but I can do one heckuva bunch of things. I always give it my best effort. Never try to shortchange anybody on anything. Make the best possible effort you can. That's pretty much been my attitude ever since I started. You rarely find that in this day and time. Not many people anymore have that work ethic. It's almost a thing of the past now. I don't know really why things changed; I simply always accepted it as the norm. Apparently, most people didn't. Whether it was a menial task or the most sophisticated task you could find, I give it my best shot and it's always served me well.

I had a pretty good job there. I was top electrician. Took care of the battery formation equipment, which they later computerized. This boy and myself took care of that as well. When somebody got in deep trouble someplace and needed assistance, after a reasonable length of time, if they hadn't resolved the problem, the boss would usually send this fellow and myself to see if we could assist. Sometimes the job was easy, sometimes it was difficult.

When responding to the general question, "Can you tell me about your job," the narrators quickly moved to the subject of the health and safety hazards in the plants. With their dramatic and detailed cataloguing of the dangerous conditions in which they worked, they conveyed what to them was the most distinctive feature of their job—that it was physically demanding and required a level of intelligence and skill just to, as Phil Nalley of International Harvester put it, "leave out of there every day like I came in pretty much." The first set of narratives that follow conveys the heat, noise, and other dangers at International Harvester.

Rob McQueen, International Harvester

The dangers of some of the jobs was unreal. They had tours; they would bring tours through. They would never, ever take anybody up to core knock-out. That's where I worked a whole lot. You worked a half-hour on and a half-hour off. You'd try to cool yourself down, collect your breath. You were swinging a sledge hammer for a half hour solid. When you hit this object that you were swinging this hammer at and knocked the sand off, that's when the heat hit you. It would rock you. Myself and Johnny Kaiser, a friend of mine—played a lot of softball with him and knew him for a long time—we worked there together. If one of us was off, it took two men to replace us for that half hour.

It was not unusual, if Johnny was off, for them to send up a couple of guys to do Johnny's half hour, and I could almost sit there and count to three and watch this man go down. It was the type of job that you had to want to work. You had to be able to work to do it. You couldn't just go up there one day and do that job. I did it for a while and it got a lot easier and, to a certain extent, I enjoyed it. I guess you get used to anything.

It was real scary to a certain extent because you had to have a cable tied to you because when you swung this hammer, all this sand and stuff went down this big hole. You're standing right in front of this big hole so, of course, if you lose your balance or something—which a couple of them did—down you went. There was people that got burnt there and what have you. It was a real dangerous job but, like I said, once I got used to it, it was just an eight-hour job. Working with Johnny, I guess I kind of enjoyed it.

It was not uncommon to see people down in the medical room—nurse's station. They had a doctor and nurses down there. When these guys would pass out up there, they would take them down there and pack them in ice to revive them. They gave out salt tablets like they were M&Ms. Eat salt. Eat salt. Now I hear they've kind of gotten away from that. I think there's a different way of looking at it. Back then, there were salt tablets everywhere. I weighed 156 pounds at six foot three and a half, and I didn't have an ounce of fat on me nowhere. I'm same height now, I suppose, but weigh 220, which I still don't feel like I'm fat. Nobody in that foundry that I know of was really overweight, except some of the older guys who had easy jobs where they might just control a line, push-button type thing. But 80 to 90 percent of the jobs in the foundry were very strenuous, very hot. You had to be fit. You had to want to work in order to get by, to survive.

The people that would ask me about International Harvester, it was always, yeah, I'm making good money. Yeah, the benefits are good. But, Jesus, don't put an application here. I'm going to quit. I need to go somewhere else. It's just too hard on you. The heat, the filth—it seems like when you work like that, and I was working a lot of overtime, the time got away from you. But the money was so good, the benefits were so good that it's awful hard to give up. There were so many times I'd say, okay, tomorrow, right after work I'm going to put in an application at Philip Morris or someplace like that. I know that you hear this all the time, oh, I'm so tired when I get off work, I don't feel like doing it. Believe me, when you walked out of that foundry, you were spent. I don't mean nothing bad by this—how can I say it—it even affects a young man's sex drive. When you got done, when you got home—it was awful hard to go home even at that point in time when I was a young man in the neighborhood of twenty-five years old. I had no energy, hardly at all. I had to strain to play with my kids, do any outdoor activities or any activities whatsoever—possibly, if I could stretch out on the couch for an hour or something like that, try to rejuvenate myself a little bit. It was rough, it was real rough.

Unless you experienced it, you had no idea what that place was like. I'm not faulting them so much for it, I could have went other places. But, the working conditions was terrible. It was the United Auto Workers Union 817 and they did everything possible to try to clean it up. But in a foundry, there is just so much you can do, so much air you can pipe in, so much soot and shit that you can pipe out. I guess I'm glad that I'm out of there. I don't see how some of them older fellows did it. I'm not a doctor but I can only imagine what my lungs looked like back then. At that time I was young and strong and fit and stuff. Things didn't bother me. After Harvester shut down, after a few weeks, I almost felt like I started feeling a little bit better. I remember waking up in the morning after having two showers, one at work and one at home to wash off what I had picked up from the time I left my locker to get to the parking lot. You'd wake up in the morning and there would be just gobs of black soot in the corners of my eyes. Your eyes just bothered you all the time because there was metal everywhere. Your eyes was full of it, your ears was full of it. They had a mask and stuff but they didn't have the respirators. Just a white thing. I know of guys that would take a sweatband and put it under their nostril, then put the mask on over that. When they would take their masks off, there was two small holes on that sweatband that was black. There again, I'm not saying Harvester was at fault for not protecting us; I can't blame it on them. It was a tough place to work. I'm sure any foundry is a tough place to work. That just so happened to be close to a living hell.

Phil Nalley, International Harvester

These huge shakers were nothing more than like a tunnel set on springs. They were on an incline and they would put these [castings] at the beginning of the tunnel. And they would bounce down and shake down through and all the sand would come off these castings and fall through the openings in the bottom and go on back down to the area where it would be reused. So you worked not only in extreme heat but with a very, very high level of noise. The ventilation that we used was just huge fans, and as this sand came out it was constantly blowing around. The temperature outside being in the eighties or nineties, whatever it was, you still wore extremely heavy clothing to keep the direct heat off of you, to keep you from burning your skin. We did things like take just a normal T-shirt and pull the T-shirt on and have the neck opening. It would then encircle your face and then you would take the arms and tie them behind your head. Then you drape the T-shirt down around your shoulders and that protects all this part of you. Then you had a respirator on and you had your goggles on. The only exposed skin that you ever had were your cheekbones. You wore gloves that went up almost mid-forearm that were very heavy, leather-welding type gloves. Even though you had steel toe shoes, you still wore a foot protector that came all the way back to the top of your foot. So, if you dropped anything on your foot, if it didn't hit the toe and it hit the upper part, it's still going to hurt. There were a lot of things that fell because of the type of motions that you had to use to swing this stuff and get it rehung.

Getting burnt was just part of the job. You knew when you walked in that day you were going to get burned some. I wore like the old Army fatigue clothing, which was real heavy cotton stuff, but this sand would hit them and it would burn holes in them. They would burn just little specks all over your arms and people would call you a drug addict because you'd have all these pock marks which looked like needle marks up and down your arms. You knew there was always the possibility that you would pass out due to the heat.

You learned very quick that you did not eat before you went to work. We worked second shift—it started at three o'clock. If you ate somewhere around eleven or twelve you'd be okay. But if you ate anything too late and you got in to work, as a rule, you would not keep it down. There were numerous days that you would drink too much water. Naturally you're thirsty, you're hot and here's this nice cold water fountain, refrigerated type water that wasn't real good for you but you'd constantly be hitting this thing getting yourself another drink and you'd learn quick not to do that. You learn to go over and get a sip and rinse and get rid of it or just swallow a sip. Do not sit there and take in three or four mouthfuls because after a period of time your body would say, "I can't do that." You'd just be physically ill. In that type of heat, drinking extremely cold water and drinking too much of it, your stomach just says, "I can't hold that much." . . . So you just learned what to do and what not to do.

There was an individual that died. We had cupolas in the foundry where they melt the iron. It's just a cylinder and they drop all the iron and the coke and everything in there and it's burning and melting and then there's a spout like a straw that would come off the front of here and that's where your iron came out. Each morning you would fire this thing up and you would get molted iron inside. Well, the night before when they shut it down your tunnel would fill up with iron and it would harden and that would be a dam so that the new iron could not come out. So you would let this thing burn for awhile and your molted iron would start eating away at this plug that's in there. So you would take a rod that was connected to a bottle of oxygen and you would light it with a torch—oxygen will actually burn at a certain temperature. And you would, there was a huge metal straw is what I'll call it or tube of mild steel that this oxygen was coming through, that oxygen would actually burn that tube. And you would take it and you would stick it back into this cupola and you would rot it out, is what it was called. Once you broke through that plug, all the pressure that's inside that cupola would come out that small hole and there would always be a huge, just flash of molted iron that would blow out up to the ceiling twenty-five or so feet, maybe fifty, sixty feet out and just spray this aisle.

Everybody was aware of it in the morning when this was taking place. It happened every morning and when you saw the attendant up there you knew what he was doing so you were aware of it. You watched because the iron's going to pop out of there and there's real, it was just a spray and it'll just sting you, it'll, like little b-b's would hit you and just burn little spots on you. So the guy rotting the cupola out, now he was completely covered with a face shield and asbestos suit and gloves and he may get a spark to roll here or there up his sleeve and get him but as a rule he didn't get burned.

This one particular morning he was working on this plug and it was proving to be very difficult and when he broke through, the inside of this cupola had capped over solid. So now you actually got a pressure being built up. As a rule it's open and it's just venting straight out of the top. Well, being this thing is capped, when it rotted through all that pressure blew out the hull and it picked up a fire brick that was three inches thick, nine inches long and three inches wide. It blew it up into his forehead and literally took the top of his head off and killed him instantly.

I know there were several others that were killed and there were generally a lot of people injured pretty bad. Burned, things falling on them, getting hit by a fork truck. The noise definitely played a factor, carelessness. The guy on the fork truck, having his job to do and doing it as fast as he could, always going to the next thing, being very busy. You're going forward and going backward and having a load on the front of this thing going backward, a lot of times you didn't look behind you; you glanced and then you took off. An individual was backing up one time and he was going all the way back to the wall and somebody walked behind him and he rammed him right into the wall and actually, I mean, it just crushed his pelvis and legs. Really not paying attention was I would say the main reason out there to get hurt. Not just you watching what you're doing but watching the other people around you. Because they're not conscious of what's going on, yeah. They didn't want to be there, they were tired, they were just uninterested, doing a job they didn't want to do, daydreaming. There's a thousand reasons I guess.

I had one injury where I was standing on a platform and I was walking backwards following this line down and the platform, I just ran out and my feet slipped off. It was about eighteen to twenty inches high and as I came down I caught my knees, one of my knees on the platform which it just ripped the skin from under my knee cap and forced the knee cap up which really hyperextended the ligaments. For about three or four weeks they put me on light duty, which was basically just sweeping, cleaning up.

The foundry as such is so hard on your body that the people that I saw that did retire, they didn't live very long. There were always problems with these people as a rule as they were getting older toward the retirement age and it was things that were life threatening. They weren't just your normal, run of the mill, got a little bursitis in my shoulder or whatever. Their whole bodies seemed to be affected. The aging process had been sped up. The company itself I thought was a good company to work for overall. Really I met a lot of people and it was an experience. It was nice to know you could go there and work forty hours and make a very nice living, but at what cost?

With explanations of how lead dust and acid can cause damage, and descriptions of their own injuries and accidents they witnessed, the employees of Johnson Control provide vivid evidence for Mike Reid's assertion: "Battery factories are dirty, filthy, nasty places."

Danny Mann, Johnson Controls

You could tell the good operators from the bad operators by the way they sweat. If they were sweating like crazy and they were running around the machine constantly, they weren't that good of an operator. It was extremely hot in there. During July and August the thermometer pegged out. As a matter of fact they had a thermometer hanging over by our line one day and I reached up and grabbed it and threw it in the trash can. They said, "What'd you throw it in the trash can for?" I said, "It doesn't work. It's been sitting on 120 for three days." It was extremely hot. You'd come out of there and your shirt would be soaked and you'd be soaking wet down to your knees. Even your socks would be soaking wet. I've watched them pass out from heat exhaustion.

You did have fans blowing and all that stuff—well OSHA [Occupational Safety and Health Administration] come in there and said we couldn't have no more fans because it blew lead dust around. So we yanked all the fans out, but you did have an overhead blower system that blew just a light air straight down on you. Those guys used to try to turn them up to get more air to blow, but the management would find out that you turned them up and they would have a fit. So, you know, there wasn't a whole lot of air circulating in there. As soon as you stepped out from under your air blower, it was just extremely hot. You're standing there working and you've got a lead pot probably the size of your bathtub at nine hundred degrees, nine hundred to a thousand degrees so you can imagine the heat that comes off that.

You could always tell the COS operators too because they always had burn marks. If they ran the COS for any length of time at all they had burn marks on their forearms from reaching in the machine and it being that hot. But you didn't touch it long because if you touched it for a little bit, you learned your lesson, you'd get scalded every time. It happened to everybody. Everybody knew you're going to get burned, you're just waiting for it to happen. You reach in there and you're trying to pull a valve out, and you can't get it out so you're kind of watching what you're doing, and your arm just touches the lead pot and, shoo! it gets you. So you just kind of shake it off and go on with it. I mean, what can you do? Stand there and cry about it? It's one of those things, you get burned, put some salve on it and tape it up. I've seen some guys really get burned bad and they got it good.... I'm smart enough not to put my hand in a piece of moving equipment. But I saw some guys get their hands messed up really good. After you do something for so long you get so used to the routine that you just do it. But one day that machine's going to bite you. So me, I like my fingers too well and I'm just not going to take that chance.

They know lead messes you up big time. That's why they did the blood test, regular lead level. They know that lead messes you up. They just don't know how bad it messes you up and how much that takes off your life expectancy, because they haven't had long studies on them. But they're paying tremendous amounts of money to pull lead paint off walls and you're standing there working with lead every day. You know, you figure. People would say things like, "Well, they're giving us these lead tests." And I said, "Boys, they're not doing that for your benefit. They're doing it for theirs." It's a whole lot cheaper to have your blood drawn and have your lead level checked than to have you be off work or get so leaded that your body starts malfunctioning and you sue, something like that. This way they can say, you know, "Well, we did all that we could do." Plus, they wanted to keep the people in there so that's why they did it. They didn't do it for your benefit, they did it because they have an operator there and they want to keep him there so, check his lead levels.

If you worked in a lead area you were paid to take a shower every night. You had an eighteen-minute shower time and you were required to take a shower to wash the lead off of you. It wasn't because that they wanted to do it because they were good guys, it's because they wanted to keep your lead count down. So they did all the tests, and then if your lead count, I think if it got above thirty and stayed above thirty for two blood tests then you went into a respirator which was bad news. It was a rubber respirator that you had to wear. When you went into the plant you put that respirator on. You couldn't take it off all day long. That thing would sweat you to death. That's why I was always very careful not to get leaded. That thing would drive you nuts. You'd be dripping sweat out the blowhole at the bottom of that respirator, it would be just dripping sweat out the bottom of that thing because it—you'd see guys, their face would be broke out from that rubber being on their face all day.

If it wasn't the lead dust it was the acid. Now, that acid tank down there, the submersion tank, you can get around that acid and you'll start itching. You'll break out like a tomato for about, I'd say, a week or two because the fumes off that acid just irritated you. As soon as your body got used to the acid, well, you kind of quit breaking out. The acid was nasty. It would burn you and it would itch you to death and if you got a cut on your hand, you get that acid in there—it would light you up! They'd run batteries down a line and they'd bring about thirty batteries in a dunker. It would drop down into a vat of acid and then they would fill and come out and then they put the caps on the top of them to send them over to work order fifteen to be charged. I was working in work order fifteen one day. You had the batteries that you hooked up in a series. If you got one of them to blow up, you don't think that'll make you jump? You're standing—you've only got about three feet between your lines and you got double deck lines, you got one of them blow up, it'll make you jump, I'll tell you that. Why you jump I don't know because if it's got you it's already got you; by the time you heard it it's too late to duck. That's what I used to tell them all the time, you know, "What did you duck for?" It's too late once you heard the bang. When that thing blew up, when I had about three of them down there on one section that blew up, yeah, I jumped. I admit, I jumped. I didn't like that part of the plant. Plus, the money wasn't there.

Charlie Noyes, Johnson Controls

My blood-lead level had been climbing for some time. It went remarkably high and I began to feel the effects: aches, pains, lethargy. You just don't feel worth a darn. It got worse and worse and I went to the nurse and she went from a monthly to taking my blood twice a month. I complained even more and all the time I'm feeling worse and worse and worse. It finally got down to the point where each one of these tests that were coming back showed a decline in my blood-lead level, but all the time I'm feeling worse and worse and worse. It had gotten to the point where she was drawing my blood once a week. I went in one morning and before work started, basically collapsed in the cafeteria. I doubled up with cramps and they called the police—didn't have an EMS unit then. The police took me to the hospital in a station wagon and I was only semiconscious. They thought I had appendicitis. They called in a team of surgeons and performed an operation, found there was nothing wrong with my appendix. Not being in a state where I could answer a lot of questions when they brought me in, I couldn't tell them what I thought may be my problems would have been, so they did an exploratory operation. In the process, they removed my appendix. They put me all back together and then the doctor, after I regained consciousness a day and a half or two days later, begins to ask all the pertinent questions. I gave him the answers and they ran a series of tests. They told me they didn't see really how in the heck I lived, but we survived that.

Buddy Pugh, Johnson Controls

Some of the scars on my arm right here, all the rest of them—when you get just a speck of hot molten lead to hit you you'll burn. It was common to everybody who was working around machines. Lead is a funny thing. When you take solidified lead and put heat to it, if it's got any kind of moisture whatsoever on the lead it'll blow out, it'll explode. And it may be just a drop on it. I've seen some pretty big explosions where there was water on the lead and nobody noticed it. But just a little minute amount of water on it would cause the lead to blow out and it would blow on your arms or blow on your face or blow wherever it hit. This lead was like 900 degrees. A big explosion would get it all over you. It would blow out all over your clothes and wherever it hit it stuck. It would burn through [work uniforms] and make little holes in them. But the clothing was protection enough to keep your skin from being burned. But now, but if you had your bare skin or your face or whatever—I was lucky enough that I never did get it on my face. But I had seen cases where it blowed out on this boy's lip one day. Just a drop of lead was all that was in there, it blew it out and got him right on the lip and he was in pain. But then I've seen other cases—in other departments, not in that department—where it blew all over this one man, all over his face one time and all that saved his eyes was his protective safety glasses.

Mike Reid, Johnson Controls

I've got a skin graft right there and right here. That was 1982, I think. So it's been fifteen years. I got caught in the COS machine. It cycled when it wasn't supposed to. One of those 1,000 degree lead pots pinned me in right there. That was my second month on my job. It probably takes, to really learn how to run that machine, it probably takes a lifetime. They had like five or six of them at one time and each one of them is different and you didn't know which one you were going to be on that night. Sometimes you would move around and each one of them is different. Some were older models, some were newer models, some had safety mechanisms that the other ones didn't. So you really had to be careful when you got on the machine that didn't have the safety mechanisms built in it. Just so happens the one that got me didn't have any safety mechanisms built in it.

A lot of people got hurt; there were a lot of injuries. A lot of burns. A lot of hand injuries, getting caught in machinery. It was probably because of the incentive because everybody was in such a hurry to get things done. And you didn't take precautions to either turn machines off or whatever. You just reached in there and try to get it while the machine's running because if you turned it off you lose production and then you get hollered at. It's probably because of the breakneck speed that we're going at and the pressure they put on you to get production. Safety was probably the absolute last thing on their list as far as priorities. Production was number one.

In the process of explaining their jobs, the narrators implicitly and explicitly assessed the companies where they worked. This assessment often took the form of a critique of management for policies and attitudes that contributed to poor conditions, and managers' lack of concern for safety or for the workers as people. These assessments contributed to the narrators' ambivalence about the job and their time in the plants. In this first set of stories, International Harvester employees express this ambivalence.

Winfred Shake, International Harvester

Harvester was good to us. I can't say nothing against Harvester. It was a good place to work. Then too, the company, they was always keen for production. Production come first, that was number one. If it interfered with any program they'd cut it out. That's why our quality got bad out there. They was hot after numbers, they didn't care about the quality of it. That's the same way with the foremen. The foremen say we're supposed to produce so much so it don't make no difference whether it was scrap or good stuff. That's why a lot of the guys didn't care. They just said, "Well, if the company don't care why should I care?" But it was management. It wasn't the company—it was management. Management hurt this plant more than anything else.

The way they done things; the way they managed things. They'd be hot on one thing and then lax on another. Like on the assembly line, rather than shut the assembly line down they'd run it without parts, running the tractors and the engines without parts and pile them up at the end of the floor. Take them off the line and well, we're supposed to build so many units a day. Well, they got the units out but they're not completed units. All right, so when they got the parts in they'd have to work overtime to replace them parts. Well, in the meantime, if they set around too long they'd get hit and everything by lifts and all. There was more damage done with them sitting around storing them because they'd have to move from one spot to another. Then too when they done the repair work there was so much damaged in taking them apart to put the other parts on. If they'd just shut the line down at the time you run short of parts then they could have started back up and wouldn't had to pay all that extra income. But see, they wouldn't be producing. If the company says we got to have a hundred you get a hundred out regardless of whether they're good or bad.

Some of it [was safe]; some wasn't. There was a lot of guards that wasn't on machines that should have been. But still I mean, some of the operators was told to do it regardless but I'd say overall it was pretty safe place to work. Of course, they were production happy so if you died they just pick your body up and go on. Push it aside if it was in the way.

Rob McQueen, International Harvester

I didn't mind the work. Looking back, I wish I would've went to Philip Morris [tobacco company] like my brother did. He's retired now. Goes out to the mailbox, gets his paycheck. I work my ass off seven days a week. I don't know if I'd still be alive today if I still worked at Harvester. I mean this sincerely, I really do. Breathing that stuff. If they was to call me back tomorrow, I would not go. If they was to open that back up tomorrow, there's no way I would go and, by the standards now, I would be making at least twice as much as what I'm making right now. There's no way I would go.

Employees at Johnson Controls employed a variety of images—being a robot or just a number most commonly—to convey the feeling that despite putting up with the hazardous conditions at the plant and demonstrating skill and conscientiousness in their work, they went unappreciated by the company.

Mike Reid, Johnson Controls

It's [the pressure] an everyday thing. The foreman standing behind you watching you all the time, that's so you didn't turn a machine off, and no illegal breaks and standing there with his watch when it's time to go back from lunch and those kinds of things. Stand there tapping his foot looking at his watch. The foremens always tried to act like they were on your side but they were all backstabbers. They'd start coming around and joking with certain people and hitting and calling them silly names and stuff, acting like they're part of the group. And it was pressure for them too. They were pressured every day. It just all trickled down, it was a trickle-down thing. They catch it; they're going to trickle it down to you.

Bob Reed, Johnson Controls

You're like a robot for one. You go in and, it depends upon what job you do but you do the same thing from day in to day out. There's no diversion in your job. You have to do a certain amount of production, they want you to run a certain amount of production, a lot of piece-work in a lot of jobs, and they put pressure on you to run that certain standard. Well, you go in and do the same job day in and day out. I mean, the same thing constantly, constantly. And you use repetitive motion for anything that you do. You're stuck in that particular area or confined area for a length of time of, in between breaks, eight hours a day. Because most people, I mean, staying in one position in one area the whole time it just gets boring. It just makes you, like I say, almost like a robot or automation, an automation robot. You just go through the motions and do the same thing all the time. Production work is fast paced, constant moving, constant doing something. They want you to work at a pace sometimes faster than what you can do, basically. The more work you do the more they want you to do and they want you to do more work with less people. If they see that you can do a job by yourself faster than two people, they'll make you do that job by your-self. They'll eliminate another person to do that. And they've done that on several jobs in that plant.

People cut their own throat because of incentive pay. Incentive pay is based upon how much you can produce in a certain amount of time. They've got certain rates for that. If you can—a lot of people speed machines up. A lot of people would run through breaks and lunch, which were not figured in certain rates. People watched their machines while they take a break and lunch. They leave the machines running for seven, eight hours. It just wasn't right, it wasn't fair to other people. The company knew it, the company even encouraged it. "Oh, we don't care if you guys watch each other's machines. If you want to do that, go ahead and do it." Well, hot summer, it's hot back in that department, it didn't even have to be that, I mean, you need a break from machinery. I mean, sure, but they said, "Well, we're getting a break." And I said, "But, yeah, that man's got to watch his three machines plus your three machines and what suffers in the process, quality. Number one, quality." That's what the company keeps preaching all the time about is quality, good material goes out of this plant so we don't lose our jobs and that Ford's happy and Nissan's happy, everybody's happy. But quality suffers because you can't watch three machines. You don't know what's coming off that machine while you're trying to run your own three machines.

I don't know how many people stacked bad-quality stuff because they want the numbers, they want the money, they want the $600.00 a week instead of $500.00. It boiled down to greed. Greed is the number one problem, I think, in that whole plant. Everybody wanted to make as much money as they could make and they didn't care how they were going to do to get it. The company knew that. They knew that these people would run as much as they could, they did everything they could to help it along. "Oh come on, Joe, we know you're doing this and that but we need production." They knew they sped these machines up. They just overlooked it and they always did for years.

If I had to do it over tomorrow I would never put an application in that plant. I would never work for them ever again. No way possible. I would never go back in that plant—come hell or high water, I would never go back in there.

Buddy Pugh, Johnson Controls

Wages was good. Hard work but I'd say most of the people made fifteen dollars to twenty dollars an hour, somewhere in that category. Everybody always complained, but I would love to have retired from Johnson Controls. You hear them complain: the work was hard and it was aggravating and it was nerve-wracking. But still you made a decent living. I made a good living as far as I'm concerned. I don't have any qualms about that. But I really had bad feelings about not being able to retire from there. When you work for an outfit that size you're a number instead of a person. They don't care.

They didn't really have the respect for people like they should have, that's the reason I say that. They had corporate headquarters and all the decisions, the main decisions, were made in corporate headquarters and they could care less about the person at a plant 500 miles away. You know, if you don't do this, you're just a number and we'll get rid of you or whatever, you know. I've seen that happen.

Charlie Noyes, Johnson Controls

When I went to work there, after the initial newness wears off, you become accepted as more or less a member of a big family. We never were a big factory, 250 people on average. Pretty soon you got to know most everybody and you were accepted. It was just like being part of a big family, an extended family sort of. After it was bought out, things began to change and that was no longer the case. Then you began to get the impression slowly but ever so certainly that you were nothing more than a number that was on ledger somewhere that represented an unnecessary expense if they could only achieve your labor for nothing.

Danny Mann, Johnson Controls

Towards the end Johnson Controls really started getting nasty and I mean, they were nailing people for things that wasn't worth it. They started cracking down on rules and things. It was such a small plant, see, there was only about 300 employees. Before if a guy needed to be off, well, at that time a foreman would tell him, "Yeah, you can go ahead and have that day." It wouldn't count against you. Well, there was no more of that. There was no more "I'm going to let you off." Now, "If you want to take off you got to take off and then suffer the consequences." There was no sick days, we had no sick days. If you were off you had to have a doctor's note. Well, a doctor's note, you can go to the doctor and get a note for anything, you spent twenty bucks for nothing. It was a whole different ball game the last three years at Johnson Controls, it was a whole different ball game. Our plant was a good plant to work at but Johnson Controls stunk. Upper management, they could care less. But I guess that's probably true in all industrial environments. You're a number and as long as you produce you're a good number. If you don't produce then you're a bad number and we take you out.

CHAPTER 3

"I Knew That Factory Wasn't Going to Last"

The heart of the former International Harvester and Johnson Controls employees' narratives of their experiences working for those plants is their explanations for why the plants closed. With these stories the workers provide their perspectives on the problems in the companies that led to the closures, lay blame for the failure of the facilities where they believe it belongs, explain the process by which the employees learned about the impending loss of their jobs, and convey their immediate reactions to it.

The story of International Harvester's financial fortunes and its tenure in Louisville was amply documented in the national and local media, which conveyed company officials' and economic commentators' views of the source of the business's troubles and the local closing. In 1977 Harvester hired Archie McCardell, an executive with experience at Ford and Xerox, to rejuvenate and modernize what the company's own leaders believed had become a moribund business being left behind by its competitors. He began a series of cost-cutting and efficiency-improving measures to shake up the company and make it more profitable. One of his goals was to eliminate some shop-floor practices and adopt others more favorable to the company's bottom line, such as mandatory Saturday overtime and restrictions on job transfers. Then, in 1979, the company took on the United Auto Workers in a protracted negotiation dispute and strike over the issues. That strike lasted well into 1980 and the consensus in the national economic press was that, coming as it did at the onset of a national recession, it damaged the company's financial situation almost irreparably. Complicating the economic picture, the downturn in the farm economy meant that customers were purchasing fewer tractors, cutting into Harvester's main business.[1]

One result of these hard times for the company was the beginning of a series of layoffs and temporary shutdowns of the Louisville facility. In spring 1982 the local daily paper, the Courier Journal, reported that the foundry and assembly plant would close for up to two months because of a decline in demand for farm equipment. A few months later, on the same page as articles on Kentucky's unemployment rate and increasing business failures, the paper reported that there would be a longer than usual summer shutdown for Harvester in the month of July. During that enforced vacation, the company announced it was considering closing part of the plant at least temporarily, beginning a long process of the phased-in closing of eventually all three Harvester facilities in the community. First, in late July 1982 citing an effort to avoid bankruptcy, officials announced the close of the assembly plant by the end of that September. At the same time officials began looking at options for the foundry. Local businessmen tried to purchase the facility but the deal fell through and in November 1983 Harvester announced it would close the foundry as well. Finally, in December 1984 Harvester agreed to sell the forge shop to Louisville Forge and Gear Works, Inc. The final days of work for International Harvester employees in Louisville came a few months later, in early April 1985, when the forge changed hands.[2]

The story of the closing of the Louisville Johnson Controls battery plant was shorter and much less reported in the local media, reflecting the smaller workforce and concomitant lighter impact on the local community. The Louisville battery facility began as the Globe Union company, which was bought by Johnson Controls in 1978. In the 1980s the company diversified nationally by adding businesses in automotive seat and other component manufacturing. The trigger for the decline of the Louisville plant, according to local reporting, was Johnson Controls' loss of the contract to manufacture car batteries for Sears in April 1994. Although plant manager Jim Dibiagio explained that the Louisville facility did not produce the batteries under that contract, he warned that the damage to the national company's bottom line could well impact the local plant. Exactly one year later officials in the company's Milwaukee headquarters confirmed that prediction, announcing that because of the loss of that contract and the "need to eliminate excess manufacturing capacity," the Louisville factory was closing effective in December 1995.[3]

The workers' stories about how and why the Harvester and Johnson Controls plants closed share some of the elements found in this reporting, but add themes that reflect their position on the shop floor and their way of understanding their work. Despite being separated in time by a decade and taking place in somewhat different economic contexts, what is striking is the uniformity in theme if not in detail between the stories of the closings of the two companies. Perhaps it might be anticipated that the former employees, in their version of events, exonerate the workers and the union from responsibility for the closing. They emphasize the quality of their work and their dedication to producing for the company. And, with few exceptions they insist the union did all it could to prevent the closing. While conceding that strikes and workplace conflict did not help the situation, they strongly deny these occurrences as the real reason for the closures. Instead, they lay blame on poor management in general and on particular individuals: Archie McCardell at Harvester and Jim Dibiagio at Johnson Controls, giving the problem a human face. Those at Johnson Controls also cited the impact of the North American Free Trade Agreement, which was adopted just before the plant closed. Interestingly, a consistent theme in these narratives is that these workers predicted the closings. They assert they were able to see the decline in the plants, read the signs in the national economy, judge accurately the intentions of management, and see through the latter's deceptions. Finally, there is a strong current in these narratives of a feeling of having been disrespected. Despite enduring the conditions described in chapter 2, performing at award-winning levels, and even working harder than ever to forestall closure, these workers believe management mistreated them not only in choosing to close the plants but in how they handled the closings.

In this chapter a small representative sample of the workers tell their story of how and why their plant shut down. Because International Harvester's closure preceded Johnson Controls by ten years, the narratives related to the experience there come first.

Howard Etherton, International Harvester

The first [International Harvester] closing was probably in '79 or '80. I think Ft. Wayne was the first big closing. They had a plant closing years ago out in San LeAndro, California, that was the first Harvester plant closing. But very few people even knew about that, it had been so long ago. Then they closed that plant at Ft. Wayne and I don't know just what year they closed that but it was either in the late '70s or early '80s. They quit making Scouts, pickup trucks and that plant alone probably had 7, 8, 10,000 people. I don't know, a lot of people. They made combines, they made thrash machines, and a lot of that equipment was made down in the plant in Memphis, Tennessee, and then they closed that plant in Memphis. They went in there first and told them that they'd take concessions, and if the city of Memphis gave them tax breaks and everything that they'd keep the plant there. After all this was done, why, they still, within a year's time, closed the plant.

Then, in 1982 we was on vacation—the company shut down the plant, not always but normally the first two weeks in July—and during that time in July they had notified several of our people not to return to work. Then on the fifth day of August of 1982 they notified the union that they was going to close the plant. It took a little longer for them to get the plant closed. They started laying off people according to seniority. Then they had a problem. They closed out that portion of the plant that used to be the old UAW 1336 and they realized that they had contracts with people on a lot of parts. They realized that they couldn't close out that portion of it and so they put 109 people in what they called the forge shop, department 53. Then that existed until April the 9th of 1985.

When we went in to negotiate the closing the company came out and said, "Well, we gave you notice of fifth of August and anybody that works on or after that date will qualify in the plant closing for the retirement at fifty-five." I stuck my neck out on a limb. I convinced the company that they knew in the first two weeks in July that there was going to be a plant closing the fifth of August and they laid these people off prior to that in order to save that many people—which was like 300 or them—of being in the plant closing agreement. The last thing we negotiated before I would sign an agreement, was they backed up and said, "Okay, these people were on vacation until the 22nd of July and we'll make that closing date." We probably had thirty-five or forty of them people in there that could retire immediately because they was already fifty-five years old. So the company did back up and make the closing date the 22nd of July, and took them people in and put them in the closing agreement.

They said the foundry was losing money, they had another foundry in Indianapolis, they didn't need both so they was going to close one of the two. Well, what they done at first, they come down to the foundry and wanted them to take concessions. When I say concessions I mean cuts in pay, considerable amounts. The people voted it down, they wouldn't take it. They said, "Well then, we're going to move the work to the Indianapolis plant." They said that they was selling a portion of the plant and they moved some of this machinery out of the plant during that time from August the 5th of '82 up until probably sometime in '84. They come in and take some of the machines out and take them to other plants like in Indianapolis, Melrose Park. Then once they got what they wanted out of it they assigned it to an outfit that came in there and had an auction and sold all of it, everything that was left.

It was real depressing. You could see the ones that they didn't know what they was going to do. You'd see a guy come by and say, "Well, I'll be talking to you, today's the last day." It's sad, really. Some of the guys you get to know pretty well. You work with them day in and day out, for instance I had twenty-eight years when they closed the plant, a little over twenty-eight years and I knew just about everybody in the plant by the fact that I was a union official. Hell, you could tell, some of them had tears in their eyes. You could tell they didn't have any idea what they was going to do. You work today and tomorrow you don't have no job. One wanted to blame this one and one wanted to blame that one, that the company, bad management caused us to lose our jobs. Then another group said, "Well, it ain't that, it's because we got so many damn different unions in here." I'm sure both played a part in the closing of the plant. In 1979, we had over a six-month strike that went into 1980. I'm sure from that day on they were probably discussing—the company—what to do with the plants, that they couldn't operate the way they were and so forth. I'm sure that before we got a closing notice in 1982 the company realized that two or three years in advance, that something like that was going to have to happen.

We talked with the company on a weekly basis. Even the 109 people in the forge shop gave up all of our cost of living raises, we gave up some of our paid absent days in order to try to keep the plant here in Louisville and it still closed. The last ones that was there of the 109 people, who were there until April 9 of 1985, we worked on April 8 of '85 and they sent us a telegram at home not to come in the next morning. The plant had been sold to Jim Payton, I believe is his name. It really hurt the people that was there. What they said was they was afraid that we would sabotage the plant if they waited until we worked the 9th. But to my knowledge, there never was anybody ever sabotaged anything in the plant during the layoffs.

I don't know what caused the closing. Economy, I don't know if that caused it. Ford Motor Company survived, General Motors survived, Chrysler survived. Another thing that's important is, back several years ago under the Reagan administration, the Chrysler plant liked to went belly up. The federal government went in there and made them a big loan and the employees all took concessions. And look what the Chrysler corporation is doing today, they paid back them loans, they gave back their employees their concessions they took. If International Harvester could have got that help it's a very good chance we'd still be selling International Harvester tractors and also combines and cotton pickers and everything that they don't make at all now. I don't know how many thousand people work with the Chrysler corporation but several thousand people are still making $22.00, $24.00 an hour. It wouldn't have been if the federal government hadn't loaned them the money to where they survived. I never understand why they didn't for a company as big as International Harvester right away, because in 1979 Harvester had 43,000 UAW people alone, so they were a big company.

We tried to get meetings with the governor. Not only did I, all the union officials in the plant. We finally got one meeting with the mayor's office, you know—not him but somebody out of the mayor's office—and, of course, we were told that there was nothing that could be done about it, that the plant was already up for sale and they wasn't anything that could be done. We thought they could do the same thing that they done with a lot of other plants. They could step in and give the plant a break in taxes and so forth just like they do a new plant coming in here, and possibly kept a portion of the plant there. That guy Payton is still running, he probably works 150 or 200 people. If that many jobs could have been kept here, local people, of our people, why, that's what we wanted to do. We didn't get any help from anybody.

Don Anderson, International Harvester

In '77 or some place along in there they hired a new CEO. He promised them he would show them a huge profit, and if he did they would give him several million dollars. I forget what it was, I don't remember how many millions. So he took over the reins. Where we used to produce enough inventory to keep each machine going for three or four days in case operation one shut down, well, he come in and said inventory is gold, and he shipped all the inventory out. Now if operation one goes down all four lines are down. That particular year he showed them a tremendous profit, I think it was 160 million or something, it was a huge profit.

Then, the CEO made the announcement he was going to break the union. He was going to go in and take away a lot of benefits, just so many benefits, so the union went out on strike. It was '79. They wanted to take away from the workers but that's after posting this huge profit. That's when we struck. We were out for about nine months to a year. When they finally settled the strike they didn't take away anything and they still gave us the same percentage increase. Then in '80 they posted the worst earnings that they've ever had but they still gave the CEO his millions of dollars that they loaned him. They agreed to give him this money on the profit that he showed. Well, they forgave him of all this loan, and then they fired him. Harvester was just about ready to go bankrupt by this time. We were all trying to go back to work and they started phasing everything out then and I think, well, the rest of it is history.

I think it was a combination of factors where they made such a huge profit and then they come back a year later and they want to take benefits and money away from the workers and they fought pretty hard over that. When they finally decided to settle they were already broke, all their profits was gone. But it was just one of those things that they wanted to break the union and they couldn't. Some people look back and they do blame the union for the strike. But then on the other hand, if you take the overall picture, just about a year before the strike the company posted the largest profit in the history of Harvester's life from the McCormick days to International Harvester. That's why the union or the employees were so adamant that they were bound and determined that they weren't going to give up anything. They still wanted to get a raise.

I think 1980 was when the first rumor started flying about them closing. I thought they would never really close the door. They were cutting back, laying a bunch of people off, and I thought, "Oh, they wouldn't get to me, they'd have to shut the doors to get to me." I didn't really think they would get down to that point because here they had spent I don't know how much money to put in an electrical substation to supply more power for the plant, and they put in all these computerized machines. They spent all this money shipping all this stuff in and hooking them up and training us to work on them, on-the-job training by the way, and I thought, "Surely they're not going to shut it down." The particular line that I was on they were producing about eighty to ninety parts a day without any major problems. Another plant of Harvester, they could only get about twenty-five to thirty a day of the same product. They even sent them down here to find out how we could do that. But they still shut us down. I'll never understand how a company can work that way, shut down a plant that produces eighty parts a day and keep another plant open that only produces twenty-five.

They told us at that very first time they started laying off everybody, that the reason was that they were cutting way back and only continuing the operations up in the northern part. There was a plant in Ohio and a plant in Indianapolis and Illinois, Rock Island. That's all that they really told us. So they shut us down to consolidate more up there. They were going to move all the operations up there to one of those three plants and phase this one out, and as soon as they could sell the forge division then they would close it up.

The foundry, when they shut down, they just laid everybody off and they never called them back. But when they went in the forge division the work started picking up, so that's when they called me back. They had more work to do in the forge division. That wasn't my favorite place to work, but it was still doing electrical work. They moved everything out of the main plant, the machine division. We knew it was going down, we could see the UAW production workers were leaving quite a bit. Of course, they kept us on to disconnect everything. We were disconnecting everything and helping them to put it on a truck, a big semi-truck and hauling it off and so they needed us. I still thought, "Well, they're just moving out certain ones, and it's not going to affect the whole plant." But after six months or eight months it kind of hit me, I said, "Oh boy, it is going down because it looks like we got an empty building here." As soon as we started getting about 90 percent of the machines out of there they just come in and said, "Well, now we can see that we're going to have to lay you off by the end of the week."

Then after that they did shut the doors for us. I was on second shift and that's from three to eleven. We would come in anywhere from a half hour to five minutes early. I went in about a quarter 'til and I'd punched in and was heading up to change my clothes, and they said, "Go upstairs and wait around upstairs, don't change clothes, don't do anything, don't go anywhere, just go upstairs and sit." So we did, and about an hour later they came in and they says, "Well, everybody leave, they actually sold the forge division." The new people wanted everybody to be out of here. I said, "What about our tools and what we've got in here and any personal clothing that we might have upstairs?" We just walked in with what we had, and we changed. "No, no, just forget about all that and go on home and come back tomorrow." The next day I went back to get my tools and my work shoes and work clothes that I had left up in the locker. We kind of knew that it was coming but we thought it was a rather strange way of doing it. When I went back, two guards whom I knew from being out there for so long, they walked around with me, and they kind of thought it was a joke too but that was their job. They had to follow me around, and not stop me from going anywhere but just follow me around. I went around and picked up everything that I had up there and cleaned out, completely cleaned out everything and went on out the gate and put it in the car, and they never said a word. They were scared to death we were going to sabotage something. I talked to one of the guards, I guess it was a couple of years later, and he told me, he says, "They told us that the employees were going to steal the place blind and sabotage the place. But y'all was very orderly, everybody, all the union employees." The management people stole them blind. It wasn't so much the closing as in the method that they used.

I was disappointed because I had hoped to retire from Harvester and I thought that the city and county government could have talked to them to see if there was anything they could do to keep the doors open. Jefferson County and the city of Louisville didn't even talk to Harvester about what they could do to keep the plant open. But as soon as there was some rumors that GE was going to move, well, Jefferson County went out there and really made a big show of what they were going to do for them. There may not have been anything that the county or city could have done but what I heard they didn't even do anything. That kind of got me, they didn't even talk to them. I don't know what the details were but I think they did interview somebody from the government, and they said, "Well, we didn't even think about it, talking to them." That might have been, because I don't think it was ever thought of before then. I wasn't too upset at that time. It was later when I started finding out they started doing all these other companies, so why couldn't they do something for Harvester? But it was too late then.

Rob McQueen, International Harvester

In a place like that, you learn through experience that there's going to be a layoff next week, and then it doesn't happen. Matter of fact, every week there was some type of a rumor. And, yes, this rumor came through but everybody laughed about it, especially myself. I said, "This wouldn't happen. They just put in all this money in this foundry. There's no way they would close it down." I didn't pay a lot of attention to it. I guess I wouldn't let myself believe it. I was kind of looking for a break. When you're laid off, they added to the unemployment check. So I finally did get laid off, and I never went back to work at International Harvester. God, I remember being so scared. It was almost like when I first walked in there. I didn't know what I was going to do next. At this point in time, there was no more jobs out there for just anyone. None of these places—the railroad, Philip Morris, GE, LG&E—was hiring then. It was just such a shock. Nobody was prepared for it. It was almost like an airplane crash. You don't prepare yourself when you get on a plane for it to crash. It happens [snaps fingers], and that's pretty much the way that was.

I often ask myself [why it closed] and I have no idea. They opened up production instead of making third shift just the clean-up shift. There was quite a bit of production being run on third shift. From the time that I hired in to the time that it closed, it seemed to be a hell of a lot more stable when it closed down than it did initially. They were putting money in it. You could *tell* they were putting money in it. At this point in time was when I first started hearing about robots doing men's work and possibly taking over the workforce. Computers, automated lines, this was just coming into the world, at least my world. I started hearing about this. Well, they came at Harvester and put one in. Spent a bunch of money on it. It would usually take, I'm guessing fifty to seventy-five people, to do the same thing that this automated line did, that only took eight to ten people to run it. The cost—of course, it's just hearsay—a million or whatever. You could tell by looking at it, it was tons of money. So that was kind of like a security blanket for a lot of people. They're finally doing something to this old foundry. Even though that wasn't really the way we wanted it to be, because of course that cost a lot of jobs. But yet, it was also security. If they're going to put in this kind of money here, this place is here to stay.

I don't even remember the reasons that they might have given to the news media on why they closed. Maybe I'm biased but I thought there was a lot of piss-poor management. They started running a lot of second- and third shift lines. They would hire these foremen, and all they was worried about was that Robbie met his quota of 300 pieces, regardless if 250 of those they had to trash once they got down to the end of the line. So then he went up to his general foreman and, "Well here I got all mine out." But, hell, it was all trash. It was a shame. I guess it's corny. Sounds like my father and my grandfather always beat in my brains, "If it's worth doing, it's worth doing right." I remember so many days of running trash, and I knew that I was running trash, but yet being told to run trash so I could make my quota. I was making my money, regardless. I would get so much for so many pieces. But 75 percent might be trash because I could not get a machine fixed or pattern fixed or whatever it might be. But I run my quota. My foreman's happy. He's patting me on the back, "Good job, McQueen." Yeah, I guess so. So I think there was a whole lot of that.

Harvester was not going broke because of the union or they wouldn't have been able to afford these automated lines. I am not trying to pull the wool over your eyes. That is just my feelings. If I thought that the union had something to do with it, I'd say, "Yeah, we got too greedy" or something like that. I just don't think that was the case. I believe that a lot of the city of Louisville thought we was making so much money—which we was making pretty good money—but these people wasn't in there. They wasn't in there swinging these sledge hammers and getting burnt by iron and pouring iron and watching it spill and looking like the Fourth of July right beside you. [When] that iron hit that floor it just exploded. They had to pay people pretty good there. They had to. But I think that people thought that because we was striking quite a bit, that we were—there was so many times I'd be someplace maybe at a bar or something. "Where'd you work, at Harvester?" And I'd say, "Yeah." "Well, you all got that place closed down." "What are you talking about?" "Well, hell, you all was always striking and, hell, you was making good money. What do you need to strike for and stuff?"

I have a bad taste in my mouth for International Harvester. I really feel like there was something shady or something going on. I don't know exactly how Louisville Forge turned around and opened up. There was no way I could find out who at Harvester was maybe having some control of that. Is Louisville Forge the type of thing of, "Well, we closed it down but we're going to open back up as Louisville Forge and pay these guys a hell of a lot less money to do what you guys was doing?" So, yeah, I feel like they did the community a hell of an injustice. I find it hard to believe that they could put in the money and the way things was going and then just all of a sudden it's over with. What kind of tax break did they get? What kind of insurance rebate did they get? You're talking about a multimillion dollar operation just [snaps fingers] boom.

Phil Nalley, International Harvester

The *Wall Street Journal*—it was 1980 or '81—quoted the CEO or president of International Harvester as saying that he would close Louisville works because of the strike that we had gone through. We had gone on strike for six months. The UAW, which represented also Ford Motor Company and your big automakers, they had years ago allowed the automobile industry mandatory overtime so that they could keep up with production demands. You know, naturally in the fall when your new model comes out there's a need for overtime. So they made it to where you had to work ten hours a day, six days a week, as a rule. International Harvester wanted to do that in line with what the automobile industry was doing because they saw it naturally as cost effective. You can hire less people, you pay less benefits. He wanted to bring this to International Harvester. A lot of the other locals out there, being as it was a nationwide strike, they were willing to accept this. They were small areas or their jobs weren't that demanding. Well, if you worked in the foundry, the thought of having to work ten hours a day or on that sixth day, that was going to be pretty tough. It was hard enough getting in there five days a week. So naturally they wanted to use this overtime in the warm months when your fuel costs are down, your transportation, everything is at a lower rate. Well, that's the hardest time of the year for us to work. So we held out, we would not agree to the mandatory overtime. The company tried a lot of different tactics to bring us back in. There were court injunctions. Everything that you can think of within a strike. It was very lengthy, started in the fall and went into the spring. And the Louisville works was very vocal in keeping this issue alive and not allowing them to get it. The strike really affected International Harvester. International Harvester supposedly lost $228 million dollars or something over that quarter, the first quarter that we were on strike, and they had posted record profits the quarter before we went out on strike. So naturally it was easy to show that they had lost, had record losses. It's one extreme to the other. Yeah, it was a long, long strike.

So when it came time to sign the contract or ratify and sign, that's when you heard this rumor, you know, "Yes, you did win, you won the battle, but I will win the war," is basically what you heard. Well, what's that mean exactly? What terrible thing is going to happen? He got even is what he did. I never met the man and there were times I wanted to meet him because for someone to treat people that way just because they can don't make it right. Sometimes you have to answer for those things.

In the article it said that he was, as a bonus, he was lent $1.2 million dollars. If he brought International Harvester to the competitive numbers that Case and Caterpillar were doing—which were the two big companies within the farm implement business—if he brought their numbers up into that range, this loan was forgiven. Well, he went the ruthless side and decided to cut the maintenance aspect of the plant and that's a quick way to show numbers. To lay some people off is another quick way, and you can offset your production numbers pretty easy. In this article it was talking about how the company basically made the mistake by giving him the free rein and saying "Here, do it." There weren't any checks and balances in place to make sure he did the way he was supposed to do it. And in that article it also talked about how he said that he would close the Louisville works. That was a real sore spot with the stockholders and the board because they had put all this money in here. They had just spent twenty-eight million dollars in the foundry bringing a new line from Germany and installed it in the foundry, and running at the 40 percent capacity it was already outproducing some of the older lines running at a 100 percent. So this thing was really, once it got to speed, going to be a boost for the foundry here in Louisville. And now it went into mothballs and just sat there. So they kind of admitted that they had made a mistake.

So then you start seeing that what you've been hearing as rumor is actually becoming reality. Each time they would do a layoff they rolled everyone. Your foreman would come to you one day and say, "You've been rolled by so-and-so. Come on to the office." You would go, and there would be a list of jobs. If you had more seniority than that person that job was available to you, and you would pick the person that you wanted to roll. So it was kind of like the domino effect. This happened about six or seven times to me over the life of the [closing of the plant]. There were the brief moments where, for whatever reason, they would pick up just a little bit in production, and some of these jobs would open back up again, and people would move back up, which would allow you to move again. Then maybe that lasted three weeks or a month, and then that job, all of a sudden they would reduce the numbers again, and you would roll someone again. So anyway, you're watching this actually happening, and you're hoping and praying that it doesn't, that for whatever reason someone decides that this is not right for the Louisville works, and they're going to keep this place open. After they made that announcement, it seems like about a year and a half before I lost my job.

I think the economy played a—well, no, not really, forget that. I actually think that it was the vendetta that this individual had. Times were rough all over; I mean, people weren't buying cars or refrigerators or washing machines or homes, but as far as a total closing, it had to be the vendetta.

Thomas Rhodes, International Harvester

I knew it was going to happen, at least a month prior to the closing. I had hints of it probably a year before it happened, some of which came from the plant manager. That's another deal in itself. I had worked in '81 with the United Way with him. To say that I became good buddies or close friends with him I'm sure would be an exaggeration. But we became friendly on a talking-by-name basis and had a few drinks and dinner together, because he was very much involved in a campaign and believed in it strongly, which was a whole lot better than the manager that we had prior to that. They didn't give a damn one way or another about the city. But he was more involved in that, and as a consequence came to a lot of these board meetings and things like that, which allowed us to socialize to some degree. Anyway, after the long strike in

'79–'80, in '81 he told me on two or three different times, not point blank what was going to happen but suggested that was a very realistic possibility. I'll put it that way. He didn't actually say it would happen but basically told me to be looking, see what was going on because he felt like it was inevitable that it was going to happen. I don't know if he was telling me that because he respected me and liked me—I hope and I think that was the case—but he was saying that nevertheless.

It was pretty much known, I believe, that it was going to happen by the community leadership, Chamber of Commerce, people like that. It was a known and planned deal several years prior to it. When I worked for United Way I was in and out of the Chamber of Commerce facility several times and saw the architects' little models of what they proposed for the city in planning and zoning. I saw that at that time they were looking at making the airport larger. Of course, the foundry literally backed up to the airport. The airport was built because of the plant being there to build airplanes. The powers to be, being the prominent people of this community and the leadership, did not want a dirty, old, smoky factory there; they wanted to make a pretty place out of downtown. Their idea was building these skyscrapers and building this wonderful airport. A lot of the people don't know that and I'm not trying to toot my horn, but I just by chance happened to see it.

I think that strike probably helped to drive the close. Yeah, to say that the strike had nothing to do with it I think would be very unfair—but to say that the company's primary focus was no longer in agriculture equipment but was in trucking and diesel engines would be very accurate. I don't know how diversified you realize the company was but they were quite. They were involved in turbine engines, they had a steel mill, Wisconsin. Steel was there and they owned that, plus fourteen plants, several warehousing facilities. They were quite diversified. In fact, they held all the major agricultural equipment patents in the world. The company was 150-something years old when it shut down. They were the Cadillac of the agricultural industry. They were the number one seller, they were the number one innovator, they were number one period. Did the strike have anything to do with [them no longer being in the business]? I'm sure it did to some degree. To what degree totally I can't tell you. I do know that there was during a period of time during the Carter administration—not that Jimmy Carter was primarily, necessarily involved or was the cause—but we had extremely high interest rates, high teens and low twenties, mid-twenties. Their intention without any doubt in my mind was not only to cut a lot of salaried jobs but to try to destroy the union. It was made pretty damn clear. I don't think there was any question in anybody's mind what their intentions were.

I read quite a bit. I used to take two particular business publications, *Fortune* and *Forbes*. I've read articles in both of them that determined International Harvester being one of the worst managed companies ever in the history of this country because of the things that they had done. They had gotten out of the Scout business, it's like the sports utility vehicles. It was one of the original ones, only it was a heavier duty built vehicle. They also made pick-up trucks. They got out of those businesses, they got out of the agriculture implement business, they got out of the turbine business. It was up on top and then all of a sudden a lot of the businesses which were the heart of the [company] were no longer in. I think this plant closing here was a combination of, in my opinion, very bad management to allow the agricultural equipment business to slip away like it did. Their main competitor at that time was John Deere, which now is the top of the heap, and they didn't go out of business, they've made money ever since then. But I think they chose to get away from it for whatever reason. I think they made some extremely bad decisions in business especially in doing away with that Scout when they were just beginning to get hot. In my mind it was very poor management because it's turned into probably one of the most lucrative businesses within the automotive business ever in the history of time. Short of the Model T maybe.

But, yes, I think the strike had some bearing on it too. To say it was the cause of it, I'm not saying that because I was a union member and involved in it. I think that sure it had some play on it. I mean, you were going through bad economic times, we were off for six and a half months, product was not being built and shipped, the parts were not being built and shipped, we're losing business. Did the strike cause that? Yes and no. I mean, it's a two-way street. If the company don't want a strike you're not out there to start with, and anybody that doesn't believe that is crazy. Because unless it's some totally unrealistic demand they have the choice to make. I mean, in that case it was not. Harvester was out to break the union, and it was very well known. It's not something that I'm saying or assessing on my own, it was very clear that's what they were doing.

Anytime you stay out that long nobody wins, you really don't. When you stay out that long there's a lot of people that get hurt. Some of the smart ones probably get by for two or three years but the average Joe probably three or four months if they're lucky without any income or almost no income. Had it not been that my wife worked at Ford we would have been one of them. We were in pretty good shape. We never really went without but it was because she worked and made good money. A lot of people lost homes and things even then because they got so far behind. There's a lot of people living paycheck to paycheck. Yeah, the strike had, it played its part, there's no doubt about it. It played its part in a lot of ways. But primarily from the loss of business, especially probably service parts.

But, there were a lot of things that happened prior to and after the strike. They had hired not only this McCardell to come in, who was a CEO of the corporation, but they hired a company that were supposedly cost cutting specialists. Their big deal at that point in time was having too much inventory of anything, literally anything. In fact, they went through the plant when they first came in and put these little posters up of the inventory, and you'd see them everywhere. Which is true, it is money. But I think they went too far, too fast, and cost that company a lot of money. It got to the point where we would have shortages. It was the beginning of this "just-in-time" type thing. They were taking the inventory out and there was no access to parts. That's like cutting your finger off and wondering what the hell happened to your finger, you know. It just didn't work.

So I think yes, the strike played a part but there were many other factors that were just as strong. I don't think the city wanted it to happen, but the other side of it was that they would have had to change dramatically the rest of the plant and bring something else in to operate. Because you don't build tractors if they're not selling them. But now, the forging facility was very valid and very valuable, and the foundry had just been renovated to one of the most modern foundries in the country. Certainly much more so than the one they kept open in Indianapolis, which is a dirt-floor facility that's over a hundred years old. My suspicions are since there was little done or nothing that they didn't really have the interest in it. I think their idea was to get rid of these old redneck smokestack places. They didn't want them, that's not what they wanted in their city. They wanted to make changes to more modern corporate centers, and that's still the direction they're going in. From the company standpoint, at least part of their standpoint, they would have to have practically redone that plant and bring some other type, something truck-related into the facility. At that time they had the plant in Springfield, Ohio, and then their largest plant being in Ft. Wayne, Indiana, which at one time had well over 10,000 people. So it would have required them to do something with one or the other or some part of one or the other or both to justify bringing in this place here.

After the long strike in '81 when they came back with this concession contract and our people accepted by not a big majority, but it was accepted. I think the union and the people of the union made some terrible mistakes by ever going along with that. I think they should have turned it down. They should have voted it down. I don't trust companies, I truly don't. And the reason I don't is because they've taught me not to. I knew that even though they were threatening to take bankruptcy and they were going to go out of business and all that, I knew and understood enough about the company that they were still paying stock dividends to major stockholders, so why should I believe the company was going to go broke? [They treated workers] very poorly because they lied to people. They told them that if we took this concession contract that they'd keep the plants open, they would take this 300 million dollars that they were saving and invest in the corporation and make it stronger and better. A year later, not even a year later, they laid off nearly half the workforce here and in a good many of the other plants. They took the 300 million dollars and gave it to corporate executives in terms of bonuses. That's not a bullshit story—that's a fact. I'm sure there are plenty of business publications that'll tell you the same thing if you look them up.

Kenny Rhodes, International Harvester

When I got laid off I would tell you probably Harvester was one of the worst-managed places ever around. After the Harvester days I had some real good experiences in management, and I kind of more understand now some of the things they were doing. I didn't agree, and still don't agree with some of the ways they handled their finances when they were on the verge of going bankrupt, taking money that the creditors forgave and giving out over ten million dollars worth of bonuses to top management. I don't comprehend that, and I guess that's part of it that still to this day I don't understand why they do things like that. There was some situations where things that we did over there didn't make a lot of sense as far as running bad parts just to get numbers out. I felt like if you're going to do something do it right or don't do it. They obviously didn't feel that way. I guess the pressure on the foremen was to get the production levels out so they could get their bonuses or whatever it was they could get.

So I didn't understand maybe what the company was wanting to do, and I'm not even sure at that time they knew what they wanted to do. It seemed like everything that we ever were invested in turned out to be a success after Harvester got rid of it. For instance, the lawn mowers, the cub cadets, they were a very big moneymaker. We turned around and sold it out, and then it seemed like it turned out to be a rave all over the country. The big tractors, we took those out of Louisville, and I'm not even sure whatever happened to those, they started making those in Mexico and started shipping them back in. Then later on they got rid of the combines, and they got rid of the bailers and different tractor works. We were doing the little Scout—that's the same thing as a Ford Explorer—they got rid of that and now that's the biggest thing going now in America, everybody wants an all-terrain vehicle. It seems like everything they were ever involved in, once they got rid of it, it turned out to be a big deal. So I don't know if they just didn't have any insight or whether the ball wasn't falling on their side of the net. I'm not sure. I do know that International Harvester spent over 300 million dollars re-tooling their foundry, and it was the most modern foundry, from what I read, in the United States. Instead, they closed that down and moved the works to Indianapolis, which was over a hundred-year-old facility. Part of it was still dirt floors. That can't be, in my opinion, a good business decision.

But, I believe that there were a lot of things that we could have done as a team that we could have possibly—if International Harvester was even interested in keeping Louisville open—have done to maybe keep it open. I'm sure you're aware of the six-and-a-half month strike that we had, United Auto Workers had against Harvester. That situation obviously was a no-win situation, and Harvester lost dramatically, and no question we lost dramatically. That was the beginning of the end, really, as far as I can see. I believe the union could have worked a little closer with the company on some of the benefits or salary. Like the just-in-time operations where they were bringing materials in, everything the company was attempting to do, I believe that the union was trying to play against it, and I don't think that was smart. It may not have made a bit of difference, the company may still have done what they did. But I personally think that there were some things we could have done different. I'm sure really good union people would have probably said, "We did everything we could." I personally don't feel that way. I was awful close to some of the committeemen and stuff that was on some of the negotiating teams and people who said, "We'll shut the son-of-a-bitch down before we'll give them an inch." That doesn't tell me we're working together.

[In the early '80s] your interest rates on housing was running anywhere from 14–18 percent, so that means your car loans and everything else was sky high. They were closing plants in Michigan on the autoworkers constantly. People were out walking the streets looking for jobs and living under viaducts because there was no jobs. Of course, nobody really ever thought it would affect them. That was the auto industry, it wasn't the agricultural. In my opinion we're always going to have to have farmers. Of course, that's changed dramatically too. But when the strike happened I felt then that something was going to happen. They told us if they couldn't settle it and get back to work they were going to close a lot of the plants down. Now, they didn't name which plants but it was inevitable they was going to do something because they was already so many millions of dollars in the hole and there was probably no way of recovering. So I guess the company was downsizing. They just told us we weren't needed any longer. They were taking machines out, they were going to reduce employment levels and go into a plant closure. Plus what was in the newspaper about losing millions of dollars, and some of the things the company was doing like they were in trouble with their creditors. They got ten million dollars somehow or another through the creditors and then turned around and give it to the higher-ups for bonuses. To me, you can't run your checkbook like that. I mean I wouldn't think you could run a business like that. So, I pretty well felt like it was the end. Then they started having layoffs. Of course, I had enough seniority to stay for awhile but I knew when it was getting close to me that I would never go back in there again, that would be the end of it. Now, they told me when I got laid off I'd be back in thirty days. I went home and told my wife that night, I said, "I'll never see the inside of that plant again unless it's on a tour." I said, "Trust me." I knew in my heart then it was over.

I've learned since then, you know, if we'd worked together, yeah, you may have to give up something but you may gain it back, if nothing else you're going to gain it back by keeping the jobs here. That wasn't the same mentality back in those days. I'm not blaming the union for all that. I think a lot of it was the company. We would like to have done something. I don't think 401Ks were even heard of back then but something like a profit sharing. We even asked them before if we could buy stock in the company. Their answer to us was, "If you want stock in this company go find a stockbroker." They weren't intending to work with us either. They didn't care. I think that set the tone in a lot of the cases. It was us against them, just about on everything, and it didn't have to be that way. I don't think they were really interested in making it positive either. They paid you a wage, they expected you to get in there and work.

Since then, we've pretty well eliminated all the good factory jobs in the city. I mean, we got Ford, GE's about shot, we still got DuPont, what do we have left? Well, you got a lot of small manufacturing but that ain't nothing, they're not what I would consider a do-er at all like American Standard, Cohart's, Harvester. Henry Vogt Machine Company's leaving, Globe Union's gone. I think there's others but they've pretty well cleaned them out. Is that all a union's fault? No, I don't think so. I personally blame as much of that on the city of Louisville as I did anybody because they had this mentality that we're going to have all this clean air, and they didn't want their air dirtied with these factories, and I think that was a bad situation. Lost all the good-paying jobs.

The workers at Johnson Controls add an additional element to the story not present in the narratives about Harvester. Coming ten years later, the closing of the battery plant coincided with the increased public awareness of capital flight to Mexico, which, although not a new phenomenon, was associated for many workers with the passage of the North American Free Trade Agreement (NAFTA). Thus although Harvester workers noted the downturn in the economy accompanying the recession of the early 1980s, the Johnson Controls employees almost unanimously attributed their fate at least in part to NAFTA.

Charlie Noyes, Johnson Controls

Some several years before they decided to shut it down, Globe Union, the company that I went to work for, had been bought out by Johnson Controls. They skimmed off all the profits, depleted the company. They were buying one company after another and basically doing the same thing, taking as much out of the company as they could get to add to the bottom line then selling the company off. They put this one up for sale, too. They couldn't find a buyer, so there was nothing to do but hang on to it. I suppose what prompted that was the fact they had already skimmed all the easy money off and the EPA laws were being changed and environmental laws were becoming more and more strict. The OSHA laws were being strengthened and more closely scrutinized the workplace. As a result of all those things, that company was becoming more and more of a burden to them, because they had to comply with all this stuff, and it's costly to do that.

What they didn't bother to tell us was they had also built a factory in Mexico, and that factory was an increase in size. Though the company will adamantly deny it, it's plainly obvious that one of the major reasons for shutting this factory down was they could simply build the product cheaper in Mexico without the bother of all the environmental concerns. They very adamantly denied that Mexico had anything to do with it because the NAFTA agreement would require them to retrain people. But if you look at where a lot of the machinery was sent, it went to Mexico. They recruited people here to train Mexicans to operate the equipment.

A company doesn't put a division up for sale unless it no longer cares to maintain that division. They weren't maintaining the facility. Things like the heaters up on the roof, they were obsolete when they were bought and installed, which was before I came there, and it was becoming increasingly more difficult for me to keep them going. That was one of my responsibilities, was to maintain that equipment. You make request after request, you keep telling them, "I don't think I can make this thing go another year." Always, "Yeah, it'll last. It'll last. Just fix it." They're not wanting to put any money, to reinvest anything into the facility. When you see that happening, you know that there's something in the wind. It's just like your house, you can't live in it forever without making repairs. When things go bad, they have to be replaced. When you see a company not doing that, you know damn good and well somebody somewhere who makes decisions has already decided what they're going to do. So, I seen the place was going to be shut down five years before it happened. I kept telling everybody, "We're on our last leg. It's only a matter of time." Nobody wanted to believe that but I seen it coming.

Another one of the things that brought about the demise of this plant locally was a contract that was negotiated with Sears. We had made Sears and Roebuck's Diehard batteries for years and years and years. Ever since the Diehard came into existence, we developed them. Prior to the closing of the factory, Sears wanted to renegotiate because the contract was up. It was my understanding that Sears had asked for a reduction in price of a dollar or more a battery, and we were selling to them very competitively to start with. They wanted absolute, sole control to the proprietary rights in the development of new technologies. They didn't want that shared with any competitor. They simply asked for a lot of things that it was obvious, with any good common sense, they had no reasonable expectation of ever achieving. So it's pretty apparent they wanted out of that contract because they had been offered some of those things by a competing company. The long and the short of it was, we couldn't concede to all those demands. They gave the contract to a competitor. Now they wished they hadn't. This other company built them cheap junk, and it obviously took a toll on their sales. They lost their business; we lost two factories. If it hadn't been for their stand, we would not have closed this factory in all likelihood.

Danny Mann, Johnson Controls

Johnson Controls diversified so much they started losing their tail end. The battery division is what kept them afloat when they bought out all the medical supply places. They about went under and the only thing that kept them alive was the battery division. But, [the old Louisville plant manager] Jim Studley wasn't good at doing any building mainte- nance. Just minimal, what he had to do. When the new plant manager Dibiagio come in, he said, "This damn place is falling apart." That's his exact words: "This damn place is falling apart." I said, "No kidding? What was your first clue?"

We all thought when they brought him in that he was the hatchet man because he had just shut a plant down. So when he came here he asked everybody if they had any questions, and I asked, I said, "Yeah, I want to know if you're here to shut this plant down." His answer was "No, I'm here to turn it around." Well, lo and behold, he was there to shut it down. But he told me after that meeting was over—I introduced myself as a union rep and all that—he told me, "I will not go through another plant closing. I've done it once, and I'll never do it again." Before the plant closed he shipped out, and they brought the old man- ager back in to shut the plant down. I think Dibiagio told them he was not going to shut that plant down. He was not going to go through that again, because it's an ordeal to really shut that thing down. I'm sure it works on your head just the same as it works on everybody else's head. You're watching these guys who've got forty years in this place and you're yanking their bread and butter off the table.

I'll tell you what, now, the way I feel about him, if they buried him I'd go up and spit on his tombstone. He was good and for the first six months I believed him but then I started seeing little things. I started getting on him big time and everybody's going, "Man, get off his back." "No, I'm telling you guys this guy is a snake in the grass. He's a viper waiting to strike." I could tell by the way he was operating. I could see it coming. Then when he come down asking us to go on seven-day-a- week continuous operation—no overtime, which means that you was going to have three shifts and somebody was going to get stuck work- ing Saturday and Sunday every damn week for straight time—I said, "No, it'd be a cold day in hell before I do that. I'll lose this job but a man has got to have some pride."

Then we heard there was going to be another plant shutdown, but they didn't know which plant it was going to be. After they shut Dallas down and all that and then they shut the Bennington plant down. Then he came to here and after we talked, had a few meetings and stuff, that's when I wrote on that calendar, I said, "This is when it's going to be, they're going to shut this plant down." I could just tell by the way things were going. Nothing being bought. All these plans they had for new equipment weren't coming in. There wasn't any money being spent on the building, not unless it was absolutely necessary to spend that money. There was just little things that just gave me hints. There were probably about three or four of us standing up there that were just a little bit more intelligent than the rest of them and watched, and I said, "The writing's on the wall, man." Not that we were any more intelligent, it's just that we had our eyes open. These people were wishing for a dream. Well, I'm not an optimist, I'm a pessimist. Some of the statements that he made, that Dibiagio made, really made me think things. He said, "They could spend six million dollars in this plant and not get it back up to snuff."

The Louisville plant always got the hardest batteries to run. If the other plants couldn't run them they sent them to the Louisville plant and Louisville would make them work. We could make those batteries run. Ford, they were tough, their specs were really tough. They checked a battery off the truck and if that battery wasn't exactly what they wanted all of them would come back. We had awards from Nissan and Ford and Toyota for zero defects. So that means everybody's doing their job. We built a good battery in Louisville. They sent Caterpillar batteries down here to us. Nobody else could run those batteries because Caterpillar was tough. They were huge batteries, 8D batteries that weighed 136 pounds once they were built full of acid. We ran those batteries, and we got numerous awards from Caterpillar over the quality of the battery.

Now, this is all hearsay but Sears wanted more competitive costs. They had been building Sears for shoot, twenty-five years, thirty years I guess. But they never did really have a contract with Sears. Then Exide started coming on very strong and built a couple new plants. The Japanese bought Exide out and started just pumping money into Exide, and they had money to spend. But they negotiated with Sears for a month, maybe two, trying to keep that business, and finally Sears got down and said, "Well, we don't want you to build Walmart batteries." Well, shoot, Walmart was selling as many batteries as Sears was. But if everybody, if you ask the average person on the street, name me a battery, they'll say DieHard because of the marketing campaign that Sears did. I guess Johnson Controls got fat and happy and started taking it for granted but then Sears started asking for unreasonable demands. They wanted the right to any new technology before anybody else got it. They wanted exclusive this and exclusive that. Well, you can't do that when you're in business, when you're manufacturing batteries for everybody. Then we went to all original equipment, that was the toughest battery to run. So then through those negotiations Sears said, "Well, never mind." Exide was promising them the moon, and we all knew Exide couldn't do it. We had seen Exide batteries. They didn't have near the quality we had. But they were promising them the moon. We knew they couldn't deliver but Sears decided they were going to go with Exide. So that probably took the production out of two plants.

I know that Johnson Controls was wanting to get out of the battery business, that's what we were told. They had plant meetings to tell them how they were doing everything and how their business is good and all this, and I said, "Well, if business is so good then how come I read in the *Wall Street Journal* that this battery division is up for sale?" And everybody's jaw just kind of dropped. I said, "I don't read the *Wall Street Journal* every day, I just happened to pick it up, and it's in the *Wall Street Journal* that the battery division is up for sale." Like I said, they're blowing smoke again.

They told us that we were being considered, that everybody was up on the block. Then, they announced they were going to shut the Louisville plant down. They took the union representatives in there first and said, "We're going to shut this down." I don't think any of us were surprised. I mean, we all kind of thought it anyhow. We conversed about it all the time. We'd all pretty much thought that way and we weren't devastated by it. They had a plant meeting, and they told me they were going to shut the Louisville plant down and gave them a date. We all heard the hoopla all before that. Why we were being considered, why they were going to do this and that, so we had all heard that all before.

We went to Frankfort, to Governor Brereton Jones. If that guy wanted to run for governor tomorrow, I'd tell every blue-collar worker out there, vote for him. Because he was willing to bend over backwards to keep Johnson Controls here in Louisville. He had LG&E in there, and he said, "We can cut your costs" —because it takes a tremendous amount of electricity to charge those batteries—"We can cut your costs so many kilowatts." He said, "If you spend a million dollars in this plant, if you'll plant a million dollars in this building, we'll give you a million dollars in tax incentives. If you spend ten million we'll do ten million." I mean, Brereton Jones and his entourage did everything they could. I told everybody, you know, if this cat runs for senator, I'm voting for him. I met the guy, he went out of his way to try to keep that plant.

But because we are a little small potato in a great big bowl of potatoes, the national UAW didn't do anything till the last minute and then they started shuffling to see if they could do something. UAW—you can put this on tape—if you don't want to hear this you can cover your ears. They can kiss my ass because they waited too long, too late before they ever got involved. They wanted all the locals' money, but they didn't care about us. Now, the local union, we was talking about everything, just trying to keep it going, keep it alive. But the international, they waited too long. They just didn't do enough. They should have been down there beating the door. I think the international could have come down and put on a dog.

Johnson Controls didn't care about nobody but Johnson Controls, that's the only thing they care about. Which I understand that too. I'm not bitter about the fact that they've got to answer to their stockholders. But, I just felt like that everybody gave it a 100 percent effort out there. We turned that plant around, and I think the decision was already made before Jim ever got there. He's going to go down there, he's going to turn that plant around, he's going to bring them numbers up, and once they got what they wanted, they already had plans to shut that plant down. I honestly believe that.

Ron Phillips, Johnson Controls

It started out they closed Atlanta, and that was a few years back. Then they came down and said, "We need to downsize more so we're going to do Dallas, and we're going to do Wausau." Then it got down to like it was going to be between maybe Fullerton, California, or another plant. Well, everybody is doing their best to get cost down and production up. I guess it just came down to the Louisville plant is one of the oldest. We have no room for expansion. They built a brand new plant in Winston-Salem, North Carolina, and they built a new plant in Toledo, Ohio. These are big plants, probably 20,000–25,000 batteries a day capacity. We were only like 12,000 a day. We were a smaller plant, and what we made was just local businesses, the Fords and Toyotas and Nissan, which is in Tennessee. We were one of the oldest plants. Everybody there had four and five weeks' vacation. We're all making $50,000 a year, in that area, like I was making $22 an hour. So we were pretty sure we were going to be picked because Fullerton was making a little less than we was making. They had a bigger facility, and they were one of the only plants on the west coast. If they were to close them down, they'd have to ship a lot of batteries from St. Joe, Missouri to there. We had one in Portland, Oregon, which is quite a ways from there. That's when we really had an idea it would probably be us over them because we had all these plants replacing us within this area.

Then they built a big Johnson Controls plant down there in Mexico. I think it's supposed to be capable of making 30,000 a day. They asked all of us if we wanted to go down there and train these people. I said, "No, I'm not really interested in training somebody to take my job. Sorry." You know what I mean? No hard feelings, just sorry. If it wasn't for the free trade—they had to pay no taxes or tariffs to build this product down there and sell it here. They're selling the same product here at the same cost as they sold it when we made it, paying our wages. So look at the profit margin. The companies wanted them to pass this agreement so they did. Now that's open down there. They said there's a road down there that looks like a superhighway in Mexico. As far as you can see there's American plants. I blame a lot of that on the government.

If we could have proved that they were making our batteries down there, we could have sued and got a settlement. When they shut our plant down, we were making Ford, Toyota, you know we were making original equipment batteries. What they did, they took all of our batteries and they split it between St. Joe, Missouri, Toledo, Ohio, Winston-Salem, North Carolina, and three or four other plants. And they took *their* replacement batteries and sent them to Mexico. So we didn't have nothing to stand on. They didn't take our batteries, but they did. See that's the loophole. We had a petition in on it and they said, "Well, they're not building your batteries down there. Period. We know that they're building your batteries at these plants and they're building their batteries in Mexico, but that don't matter. NAFTA—that's what I blame and that's what I see. Until somebody proves it different, that's what I'll always believe.

Roy Puckett, Johnson Controls

They told us, "Here's what we want you to do, go back to each state government and see what the government will give you to keep the plant open." So everybody goes back, myself, the vice president and the plant manager, and we went to Frankfort and talked to those folks and in the meantime all the other plants were doing the same thing. When it came down to the end, Kentucky had the best offer of any of them. But they still decided to close us anyway. Kentucky offered them several million dollars in tax relief, and that was going to be offset with the employees giving something like ten or fifteen cents back of our money. Our International Union said, "No, we don't want them doing givebacks because if you do it here you'll say well, we want sixteen here and you'll go to the next plant." But the reason the state wanted to do that was because they felt that way the employees were buying into trying to keep the plant open. Also we went to the utility companies, and they had agreed to show us how to cut our utility rates and all this. So everybody was really working with us. But they weren't interested at that point. I think they already had their minds made up that this was going to be one of them that was going to be closed. I think we were picked out.

See, now we had a good relationship until the new vice president—Keith Wandell—came along. He was going to break the [UAW] council, because he figured we had too much power collectively, and he wanted to break us any way that he could. The other plants they got were of all different unions. But the bulk of us was UAW, and we had a master agreement. That way when we come down to negotiations if he tried to do something we didn't like we'd just all walk out, and then that left him with only like five plants to cover the whole United States. So we had a lot of bargaining power. This way he started chipping away at that power. Once he became vice president, when he'd come in negotiations he was always wanting concessions, but he never could back up the reason why he needed them because the company had always made a good profit. So we never would agree to concessions. Now, we told him, when it come down to plant closings, "Hey, we'll sit down, and we'll do anything to keep this plant open." As a matter of fact, I even asked him, I said, "Let me ask you this. If we work for five dollars an hour can we keep this plant open?" He said, "No." I said, "Thank you. You've eased my mind." I wanted that question answered because I didn't want it on my head that there was something we could have done to keep that plant open.

Here's another thing that made everybody in that plant mad and me especially, this plant manager come in there from Bennington, Vermont, and he'd already shut down Bennington. He told us, "I don't want to close down another plant." We'd had a plant manager who had been easygoing and didn't push anybody and the plant had really went down in production and stuff. He said, "If we can turn this plant around in production, quality and all that, we got a good chance of keeping this plant open." He was kind of the vice president's fair-haired boy, we called him. So everybody in that plant did everything that they could do. They went out. We even turned some of the lights out, every other light, people kind of worked in the dark trying to save on electricity. We did all this stuff, and they had the plants numbered in all our quality and production and stuff, and I think we came in at about number three or number four on top, and we thought, "Well, we got a chance now. We showed them we can turn this plant around." And still the decision was made to close.

I think [this new plant manager] was sent there, and I think that was to take everybody's mind off that we were going to close and build that hope up that no, we're not going to close. They felt what was going to happen, once you make that announcement everybody lays down and says I'm not going to do anything. They wanted to keep that morale up. But everybody did go out of their way and did a heck of a job to turn that plant around. People were doing extra things to make that plant look good, and they really thought we had a chance. This plant manager, he left during the night and never did tell anybody good-bye or nothing. Never even told anybody he was leaving. They brought the old plant manager back under contract and told him, "We'll give you this much if you'll come back and stay with the plant until it closes down." Because he got along with all the people. The company figured the people would work for him more than they would for the other one. I think the people kind of accepted it but those people had a bitter taste in their mouth after they were done that way and you couldn't blame them.

Buddy Pugh, Johnson Controls

I figured after almost thirty-two years, I had a pretty secure job. I think that was one of the reasons the plant closed because the average age of the people that did the work in the plant was nearly fifty years old. That was one of the reasons. It was a self-insured company, and the age of the people were getting old enough where they were going to have to have a lot of medical expenses for themselves and their family, and I think that was one of the reasons that it closed. Plus it was hard work, and they wanted younger people.

I'll give you another reason. I think that Johnson Controls was a non-union company, and we were one of seven plants that belonged to a coalition of the UAW union. They went after the coalition, and they closed down a plant here and a plant there, and finally it got so that they closed out nearly all the coalition plants. They still had union plants, don't get me wrong; but in this coalition we were in, the majority of them had already closed. We were the first people that they [Johnson Controls] ever had that belonged to a union. When they bought the battery division we were already union members. They had made their brags that they were going after the union plants and closing them down. And they did.

Another reason too was the company lost Sears' business, and Sears' business was like nine million batteries a year. I don't really know what the reason was. I do know that Johnson Controls offered them like a six dollar and something price cut per battery, and Sears wouldn't take it. It seems to me that that was kind of dumb on Sears' behalf but I don't know everything that went on. But on the other hand too, Johnson Controls' financial statement showed them making more money the last year that we worked and throughout the whole battery division than it had ever made with Sears.

Well, another reason I say was because they built a new battery plant in Torion, Mexico. They told us they were downsizing when they closed the plant but they built a new battery plant in Torion, Mexico and had just started its operations. They had increased the size of their plant in Winston-Salem, North Carolina. They increased the size of their plant in Toledo, Ohio, and they increased the size of their plant in St. Joe, Missouri, so they can't make me believe they were downsizing. I believe our politicians had a lot to do with it by having the North American Free Trade Agreement that opened up Mexico for slave labor, fifty cent an hour labor. They could hire almost thirty-four people an hour for what they paid me for one hour, and that ain't counting my benefits. I have harsh feelings toward our government, I really do. There wasn't no reason for that.

I blamed the company itself. It wasn't the workers. It wasn't for lack of production or lack of effort. They had some of the best workers in the country that worked there. I think the company just had a thing for unions, and they didn't want them. They were a self-insured company—I think they realized that the average age of that plant employee-wise was about fifty years old, and they was going to be out a whole lot of money on medical expenses in the next few years. They had a company come in and study the plants on which one to close or whatever. They didn't have to close any of them really. But they did. I think a lot of the credit also goes to the government. When they made the NAFTA agreement with Mexico, almost immediately they built another battery plant in Mexico. They shipped our jobs to Mexico, part of them. I blame that on the government. I don't think that's right.

Marilyn Reed, Johnson Controls

The plant manager that they had, they forced him to retire, and then they brought in Dibiagio, who had already been to two other plants and they had closed, so we were calling him the plant closer. He came down and they made him plant manager, and he had a meeting with everyone, with all three shifts to introduce himself and tell us his plans for the future and so on and so forth. So everyone was asking him in the meetings in the cafeteria, "Well, we hear that you're a plant closer." And he'd say, "Oh, no, no, no. That's not what I'm here for. I'm here to bring your production up." Then he brought out all these graphs and all these percentages and things and said, "Well, this is where we are and this is where we need to be in order to keep the plant open. If we don't get to this point the plant will close."

So, then everybody gets all hyped up, and we start running really good and cut down on scraps. I knew our production was bad. I knew that we would have to do better. I knew that the people's attitudes had to change as far as the quality was concerned because the consumer wants a good product now. With the times changing where the consumer is wanting a better product, we were going to have to turn ourselves and make a better product if we wanted to stay in business. I knew that. I think they really tried their best, and I think they knew we were going to close anyway. They were just trying to get all they could out of us so they could stockpile batteries until they could be prepared to run our product in another plant. I think they knew from the beginning, when he came there, but I think he wanted the best product he could get out of us in the time that we had. Because we kept saying, "Why are we having to run all this production? Why are we working Saturdays?" Because they're sending them out to other plants. They're stockpiling them in the warehouse, so that in case another plant didn't meet the production they'd have this backup.

The whole time they said, well, we would probably be the one that would stay open because we were centrally located like for shipping the batteries. We had won so many quality awards, Ford wanted our batteries. They said that they didn't want anybody else, any of the other plants to run their batteries because they had had trouble with them. But, they said that they could distribute our production out to different plants, and the other plants could handle it. The new plant in Toledo had a capacity to be able to run 20,000 batteries a day, and they were only like running half of that. They felt like they could handle the original equipment. So, they thought they could just do without us more or less.

As far as a financial situation, I think it was Johnson Controls' only option. It was a very old plant, and it was falling apart. It was easier for them to close it down than to put the money into it that they would need to put into it to make it to where it was running efficiently. They were going to go to different types of equipment that they already had in the other plants, and it just would have been too expensive for them to update us to run with the times.

Bob Reed, Johnson Controls

I've got my own theory. I think the majority of the people will agree with me. My theory is that the majority of the people in that plant had over fifteen to twenty years in there. We were all reaching the age of forty or over. We were all getting to be an old workforce. We were a UAW plant making awful good money. They had a lot of labor problems with the company because we stood our ground and we weren't going to bend to their wants. Louisville was one of the hardest plants to deal with on negotiations on contracts and anything else. We as a union got great benefits, but it took a long haul. It took all these wildcat strikes and all these walkouts and everything else to get what we got. I guess it got to the point that they said, "Well, do we need these people any longer here?"

You got to bend over backwards for the company in certain instances but you sure don't have to give up everything you fought for or worked for to keep the plant open. My gosh, we can only sacrifice so much. All the time they'd keep on saying, "Well, we can't justify giving y'all raises or this and that because we didn't make any money this year." Well, they'd have articles right there in the paper saying that they made $6.9 billion last year, moved up to a Fortune 200 company. You just can't tell people you're not making any money. I mean, sheez. But I think the biggest sticking point was they had strikes that were ungodly and they just finally probably said, "Well, we've had enough. We can't keep paying these people the wages they're getting paid."

There's been a lot of people blaming the union for the plant closing down. I've heard a lot of comments about that once I've been out of the plant. They blamed the union for not doing more than they did to keep us open, and I said, "Well, suggest how you think the union would have done anything differently. Johnson Controls had all control of what was going on." We had no indication that the plant was being closed down, we had no indication at all. So, I said, "If the officials didn't know then how are they supposed to do anything for you?" Even then, what kind of tools you going to deal with? I mean, go out on strike with them for an issue? What do they care? The plant's going to be shut down anyway. That wasn't no leverage you could use. I guess they figured they should have gotten more out of the company for them. But I really don't know what you can do. Offer more cuts in pay and then you're making the people totally mad that they're losing half their wages. Going from what, fifteen, seventeen dollars an hour down to eight, seven? They say, "I can live off of that." I've heard people say, "Why didn't they tell the company we'd take seven, eight dollars an hour, we'll still work here." And I said, "Well, that's your opinion. The majority of the people are not going to work for eight dollars an hour, not in these conditions. Not with what we have to put up with." I mean, all that lead dust, got to wear respirators, be exposed to all this kind of stuff. That's hazardous work, it really is. And if they offered that to the company, I don't think they would have bought it anyway.

Everybody knew that the plant was going to be shut down, because all the signs were telling me. They weren't bringing in any new machinery, and they weren't fixing a lot of the machinery that needed to be fixed. "Oh, put that on hold. We can do without it." The telltale signs were pretty obvious. Management would never say anything about why certain things were not being done. They were going to try to bring a whole new system in to work order thirteen because all the other plants had it. They said in order for this plant to survive, we've got to bring this new system in. Then they said, "No, Louisville's not going to get it now." So right there tells you that something is going on.

The tension in that plant was just unbelievable. People were on edge all the time. I myself was on edge every time; I hated to go in there. I had to force myself to go in every night. I could not stand going in that place every night. I think it was like that last three or four years because of all the changes going on, and because they threatened three or four years ago that another plant was going to be shut down and Louisville might be one of them. I was constantly on edge all the time. I went in there and I didn't argue with people or foremen or things like that but I just voiced my opinion a lot more. I was more agitated, more uneasy about things, and just really getting depressed. I was fearful of several other people in the plant that might physically lose it, mentally, because people were really getting to the point where they were just upset. They didn't know which way to go or do. Everybody you talked to said, "Gosh, I can't stand working here anymore. This place is just unbelievable." It's not fighting but at each other's throats a lot, and foremen and the people working underneath them, they were always arguing about things. The company was putting pressure on the foremen to get the people to produce more because they knew that the plant was going to be shut down and they didn't want to lose any production. Well, when these people know that their plant is going to be shut down they're not going to give any more than they already have. What's the sense in giving 150 percent when your job's going to be cut out tomorrow? Sooner or later you're not going to be making any money at all and you're only helping the company because they're going to take all of your production, ship it to another plant, and somebody else is going to benefit from it.

Then they said they're going to shut another plant down within a year. The union told the company that they would help them to go to Frankfort, talk to the governor, try to get better rates on different loans for improving stuff in the plant to upgrade things so we could increase our production. The company said, "Okay, that sounds good," but the government didn't go along with it. They didn't give us any rates or any incentives to stay here, which we hired like 250 people, almost 300 people, good-paying jobs, good-wage jobs. We thought if the union and the company got together and went up to Frankfort and told Governor Patton that if you give us a tax break the company will stay here. The union went with the company and said, "Okay, we'll do everything we can to keep this plant open. If it means a cut in wages to a certain extent we'll bend for that. We'll give something up to keep this plant open. We'll do what it takes to keep this plant open. We're not going to sacrifice everything. If it gets down to the bare tacks we'd just as soon shut the plant down. We're not going to give you every-thing back but we will bend with you and give you something back in order to keep the plant open." The union was more than willing to do that. That's what I get and from what the union president told us and the vice president and all the people there. Unless there was more going on that I didn't know anything about, this was what was happening.

You know, they announced it to the media before we even knew. Third shift comes into work, we didn't even know about it, we come driving into the parking lot and everybody says, "Oh, the plant's going to be closed down." It was announced over the media or through the grapevine or whatever but the camera crews were there before we even knew about it. We came into the parking lot and there they were. I said, "How about this? This is great. I've been working here for twenty-something years and this guy from channel three tells me that my job's being lost." We knew it was going to happen, it wasn't a big surprise. But, you know, golly, you owe some people some common courtesy, to let people know in advance before that happens.

Mike Reid, Johnson Controls

I knew that factory wasn't going to last. The way the place was run, the management, it was a pitiful outfit. They claim they didn't make

any money, but the company wouldn't have been there for thirty years
if they didn't make money. They were saying all this was a write-off.
We're not trying to make any money here, we're just doing specialty
products and all that. But I knew that was B.S. They were making
money there or they wouldn't have been in business. Nobody in the
Louisville division could do anything without calling Milwaukee.
They couldn't even paint the flagpole unless they called Milwaukee
and asked if it was okay. It's been that way since Johnson Controls took
over Globe Union.

At one time they had like eighteen different battery factories
around the country, and they started shutting them down just one at
a time, maybe one every two years. They started with Texarkana, I
think was the first one, then Atlanta, Georgia. There were a few others
in between. In the meantime they said they would shut down a plant,
they didn't know which one, but they're going to shut one down and
we were always on the short list. And this went on for years and years.
That was always another reason for them to put pressure on you. We're
going to have to get production up, we're going to have to do this,
improve quality, and all this stuff. We would get contracts, and we
could keep contracts. Anybody else would get them and they wouldn't
keep the contracts, places would go somewhere else. But they'd give
them to us, we'd do them, and we'd keep the contracts. We were zero
defects. We wouldn't allow any defects. We had a lot of Japanese contracts: Toyota, Nissan Mazda, Honda, all the ones that the other battery factories couldn't do. We got the Ford Q-1 Award. They put their
flag on our flagpole as quality one or Q-1.

But then we lost Sears. We used to manufacture all Sears Roebuck
batteries, and then they went to another company. That's what put the
pressure on Johnson Controls there when we lost Sears. Price was the
only reason. Somebody cut them two or three cents on a battery. That
did us in. In order to keep their little babies open, they had these little
sweetheart plants, out of these fifteen plants that are left open, they've
got their sweetheart plants that they will not shut down. So they took
some of our business that we were making that we had earned, they
took our contracts and spread them out over the other plants that were
making Sears.

What really did put the icing on the cake was when they got rid of
our plant manager that we had, his name was Jim Studley. They forced
him into early retirement and then they brought in one of their golden
boys. His name was Jim Dibiagio. When Dibiagio come in there, I
knew it that day that we were slated for closing. He came up with
some different ideas how to improve production. Okay, we were doing

more production with less people, making more money than they ever had before in the lifetime of the plant supposedly. I knew, when the first time he come in there and he gave his little speech, that we were going to be doing more work for less money and that's exactly what happened. The first thing he said we were going to do was increase production with less people. So that means people there are going to be doing more work, right? Then he came in, he cut all our rates 25 percent so that was a 25 percent decrease in pay for the same amount of product, for doing the same thing you were doing before. When they say increase productivity and increase production and all this you know you're going to be working harder for the same amount or less money. Any time they say increase productivity you've got less people doing more and making less.

He said he was going to save the plant. He was our savior. I didn't believe him from the very first start because of the way he put it out. He would talk and then he'd hang his head down like he was lying. He wouldn't look you straight in the eye. He'd turn his head around, "I'm going to save this plant." He was talking to the wall instead of the hundred people sitting out here in the cafeteria. He's got all these charts and graphs and all this pretty little designs that he did on his personal computer. From the very first day I met him I knew he was the one that was going to close this plant down, because the plant that he had come from had just closed down. Some people bought it. He was okay. He was straightforward, pretty much straightforward. Everybody bought it except for me. I think there were very few people that didn't buy it, and I was one of them. I'm trying to think of anybody else who it would have been but I knew, I just knew. There were still some people that thought even up to the last day that they were going to change their minds. Even when they saw them shipping out machinery in boxes by the truckload they still thought the place was going to stay open till the last minute.

We thought that we were pretty secure in our jobs because we had zero defects. Our quality was second to none. We all thought that's going to be the bottom line. We were productive, we were making money, the company was making money as a whole, the battery division, we were making more with less people, and here they go putting big bunches of money in for updating the equipment. They're doing all this they're not going to close. But it doesn't work that way. There was more, newer technology that they could have went with but when they didn't come in it kind of slammed the door on it. They said if you don't have these certain types of welders you're not going to go anywhere, and that was a multimillion dollar project. But they refused to put money into those welders. They said it would cost too much money and they didn't have that in the budget. Dibiagio said, "I'll get the money in the budget, don't worry about it. Everything's going to be okay." But after months and months and months it keeps going on, then you hear that all these other battery factories do have these new welders and we don't, you kind of know that something's not quite copasetic here. That was one of the signs. They are buying less now than they ever had, and they weren't carrying any inventory. Because they didn't want anything left over in there. So it kind of clued me in.

So we go on about six months, a year and everybody's production is up this much on the chart, and we're making this much more money than we ever had before, and quality is zero defects and all this stuff, and we've got contracts out the wazoo, they're going to have to hire people. Then they drop the hammer on us. They say, "Y'all are doing such a good job, we're going to close you down." That's exactly the way they put it. "Y'all made so much money, we can't stand it. We're going to have to go ahead and shut you down." That's the way it happened, that's exactly the way it happened.

CHAPTER 4

"I Was Overjoyed, I Was Sad, I Was Hurt"

During the interviews, International Harvester and Johnson Controls employees spoke of ways that job loss in the plant closings affected them. Financial hardships posed problems for many. Some lost homes, faced challenges covering bills, and had to juggle family expenses. Even when financial situations weren't dire, the change in income required adjustments in spending, both in cutting back in general and in forgoing discretionary expenditures, such as vacations, socializing, hobbies, and nonessential purchases. At the time of the interviews, several interviewees made considerably less than they had at the factories. These former factory workers commented on the weak local job market and the need for more education to compete for higher-paying jobs.

When asked about the impact of the closing many of the narrators described their subsequent careers at length. For some, their work life after the shutdown of the local Harvester and Johnson Controls facilities included time spent working for the companies at plants elsewhere. The UAW had negotiated with Harvester a master recall list, by which Louisvillians could be called to jobs in Ohio, Illinois, or Indiana according to their seniority. For those who took this option the experience was not always positive, involving time away from family, too much travel, and a hostile welcome by the employees in the new plant. Johnson Controls employees were invited to transfer to factories in other states, but without the possibility of maintaining the benefits that came with seniority. Few did so. For workers in both companies, the desire or need to stay near family and close to the community they'd always considered home outweighed the attraction of the pay and benefits they might receive by accepting a recall and relocating. Instead, most of these former employees left Harvester and Johnson Controls behind, and many of them did not again enter factory work. A consistent theme in these interviews is the satisfaction with that change in career and assertions about the positive aspects of the new jobs, despite any economic loss that accompanied the change.

The interviewees discussed several emotional and psychological effects of the plant closings. Across these interviews, narrators elaborate on mixed emotions—sometimes acknowledging the conflicting feelings; sometimes discussing one feeling and then later a different one. For example, these workers describe being both relieved and devastated, happy and sad. They also regret the loss of friends and people with whom they'd worked for many years. The closings created stress in some marriages, changes in life plans (e.g., retirement), and doubts about how to proceed. Some former employees felt bitter and/or unsettled, questioned their competencies, and wondered whether they were failures. Many interviewees expressed concern for their former coworkers, often citing examples of problems that others had (e.g., heart attacks, divorces, suicides) and through these stories illustrated the myriad effects of plant closures even if they did not experience them personally. Despite these effects, however, many reported that they had learned considerably from the experience and were glad that the plant closed. Indeed, several narrators stressed the positive outcomes the closing had on their lives and outlooks—such as preferring their new jobs—despite the financial challenges.

In this chapter we present the stories of the impact of the closings on Harvester workers first, followed by those at Johnson Controls.

Rob McQueen, International Harvester

I have no idea how to say this—whoever listens to this will think I'm nuts. I have so many mixed emotions on it. When Harvester shut down, I was devastated but yet—God, I was so happy. It was just such a hell but, yet, it was my income, it was my life. I was overjoyed, I was sad, I was hurt. Every emotion that you can feel, I think I went through it. I was relieved because I didn't have to work like that. I was hurt and sad because I was losing a lot of friends. I was losing a lot of my benefits, insurance, and what have you. But, at the same time, I was almost happy. I know that doesn't make sense but, for a period of time, I was happy. I don't know if happy is the word, or relieved. It's so hard to explain. There was just so many emotions that happened. I'm glad that I don't still work there, but, man, I wish I still worked there.

Does that make sense to you, that I was happy and sad and all this at the same time?

In another year and a half I'd be retired—I could play golf all the time. All I would have to do is walk to the mailbox and, I'm not sure of the amount of the check, but it would be more than enough to live on. It would be a lot more than what I'm making right now working. A lot more. Roughly, right now I'm making probably about four dollars an hour less, three to four dollars an hour less, in 1997 than I was making in about '82. I was probably making three to four dollars an hour more then than I am now and that was sixteen, seventeen years ago. It's unreal.

It was an important time in my life cause, to a certain extent, it put me in jail. Yeah, I can really say the closing of International Harvester put me in jail. It got me divorced to a certain extent. It was definitely the reason I went to jail. It was right before Harvester closed down, my wife and I separated. It was nothing serious such as me and another woman or her and another man or anything like that. We'd been married roughly ten years and I don't know if we just went through a lull in marriage or what. Anyway, with Harvester closing down, it was like adding fuel to the fire, I guess. Of course, money can't buy happiness but, believe me, it can sure as hell help. When you don't have to worry about paying bills and don't have to worry about what you're going to eat next or if you can afford this, whatever, it makes it a little bit easier. Well, all of a sudden, I went from one extreme to the other. All of a sudden, I didn't have money to buy a pack of cigarettes with. So, first things first, we separated. Probably if it hadn't happened—I look at it that we probably would have got back together. Don't get me wrong. I'm not blaming Harvester for my divorce. But, it kind of added gasoline on this open fire. So we wound up divorcing. But one thing I can attribute to Harvester is, right as we were getting divorced was right when all this money was coming to an end so my [child support] was based on my income then. Seems to me it was 125 dollars. No, it was more than that, 175 dollars, I believe, a week. I didn't mind paying it when I had the money.

Through the layoff, I was getting this sup-pay and it wasn't official yet that I would not go to work there again.[1] So after I stopped making this amount of money, I struggled paying child support. I hustled pool for a little while. The main thing was I went to the race track and started working with the horses, something I really enjoyed. I was making a very little bit more than what my child support was. I'll never forget that when I went to the judge to ask for a little bit of a decrease in the child support, that I'd lost my job at Harvester,

I said, "Your Honor, I'm starting at five o'clock in the morning and working till six, seven, eight o'clock at night." On the race track you do that. I said, "Here's my pay stub." I'll never forget when he looked at me right square in the eye and without any change in his voice or his looks or anything, he said, "Mr. McQueen, it looks like you're going to have to get you a second job." Right there I knew that my life had changed.

But before all that came about, though, after Harvester and after this money stopped, I could not pay child support and I went to jail. It was like nobody all of a sudden cared at all about Robbie McQueen. It was me against the world. It wasn't my fault. I was doing everything I could. I would send whatever money I could possibly put my hands on, and every other week or so I was being locked up for not paying my amount of child support. I guess you could say I attribute that a little bit to International Harvester. I'm not blaming them, I don't mean that. But, if I'd of kept that job, I wouldn't have had that problem. That was the hardest part of my entire life. I thought that when my father died and—when I was young, we spent some time in the projects cause my father had a bad heart. He had to give up his job as a truck driver and we moved to the projects. I thought that that was the hardest time in my life. It wasn't nothing compared to what it was like when Harvester shut down.

I did not have a high school education. I didn't need one. International Harvester, Philip Morris, railroad—you didn't need a high school education to get work there. If you can work, you was hired. Twenty-five years ago, whatever it was, an education wasn't nothing near like it is today. So there I was at thirty-one years old, somewheres in that neighborhood—no high school education, no job, no home, no family, as far as wife and kids. I mean absolutely no money. I had moved in with my sister. I went from having a home to having just a little bedroom that I guess I called home. I had to share that to a certain extent. She bought my cigarettes, fed me. Course, they didn't have much money neither, but she did what she could. I just could not find a job.

Finally, I find out I had a little talent playing pool. So I hustled pool for a couple of years after that. Made a decent living at it. I did pretty good. I had a gun pointed at me in Indianapolis, that's why my hustling pool came to an end. I said my life is worth a little bit more than a couple of hundred dollars. I knew then and there I had to get into something else. I was at this place where I played pool a whole lot, kind of a hot spot in Louisville of pool players. I was in there after I had more or less quit playing pool and that's where I met

Larry Edwards and his crew. I was talking to some of the crew and they said, "Why don't you come over and try [working at the track]?" So for the next four years or so, I did something that I thoroughly loved. Again, I'm not patting myself on the back, but I found I had a little talent working with horses. It came real easy to me. In a few short weeks, I was given my own four horses as a groom. And just a couple of weeks after that, I was also promoted to barn foreman. It came real easy. There at first I was scared to death of them, but it was like it was my calling. It just came so easy. I just loved it. I loved being around them, but that's another story in itself cause I finally had to quit that.

That was when [my brother] Randy helped get me this job with the City of Louisville, Metro Parks at Iroquois Golf Course; a job that I enjoy. It kind of goes back to Harvester. I can never, ever envision myself working in a plant again or going back to that. Oh, I wish I still had my job at Harvester. I wish it was still open, but yet I don't know if I'd be alive today or sitting here talking to you. This might sound a little rough, but when I left there Friday, by Sunday night and really going into Monday morning—I don't know how to say this, it's a little gross—I was still blowing charcoal black gunk out of my nose. I would leave work on a Friday and I would have a couple of days of recuperating, and I was still blowing and spitting this stuff out of my body. Even though you wore a mask and goggles and stuff, your eyes was full of metal, full of soot, your chest, your lungs, ears. You could almost look at someone and tell if they worked at International Harvester or not. It was so hard to clean yourself from that. I was there right about nine years and I didn't realize until after I had left what that short period of time at International Harvester had done to a young man that was, as I said earlier, was very fit. I was very fit and if it had that effect on me, I can only imagine what it would have on someone that wasn't into sports and didn't just get out of the military.

Now I don't make nearly the money or have near the benefits [in the job at Metro Parks], but it's clean. I'm outside on a golf course. I'm at work at daybreak. A lot of times at daybreak I've got a big cup of coffee, and I might be riding out turning on water on different fairways or greens or tees. I look over and there might be a groundhog or a deer or rabbits. There's times that I might pull over for a minute and reminisce and say, boy, this is a lot different from Harvester. I really enjoy myself at the golf course. I do wish it was a little bit more money, cause I can only imagine if Harvester was still open, there's no telling what I'd be making now. Right at the end of my retirement—there's just no telling what I'd be making.

I've been with the Parks for roughly thirteen years now, the last twelve at Iroquois Golf Course. I really care about the golf course. I have a lot of friends up there. I took up golf since I took this job. I enjoy that. I've made a lot of friends up there; a lot of guys that I knew years ago that's my age—played softball and football and basketball—we all thought that golf was a sissy game. Well, now there's quite a few of them that play golf also. Occasionally, there'll be an old Harvester buddy that will show up, so it's nice there. Of course, we talk about how glad we are that that SOB closed down, but, yet, damn, we wish it was still open. If that makes any sense whatsoever. There was so much that we missed at Harvester and so much we was tickled to get rid of.

Don Anderson, International Harvester

I think I was around fifty and I knew I was going to have to work. I mean, it was too early to retire and even if I got the retirement package at fifty-five it wasn't enough so I had to supplement. So I figured I'd have to work until I was sixty-five or sixty-two or something. So, I did. I went out with the resolve to go find another job. I was not that familiar with what seemed to me was a new system of writing up your resume. You go out there and people ask, "Well, give me a resume." "Well, I don't have one." I never had to do all that. I never learned that. I had to learn quickly. I learned that about every twenty years they changed the rules on you and then you got to relearn new procedures. Just at the latter part of your age, you do have a problem trying to get reorganized and worry about getting another job. You have to keep working.

There was one incident that I went to a company to apply for an electrical maintenance job and everything was favorable. There was three people there for the interview for the company and they all thought very favorable until they got around to asking me, "How do you like overtime?" And I said, "Well, I don't like overtime. But I have probably worked more than the average but I can't say that I like it." Well, I could tell right then that a cloud went over the whole meeting and I lost the job over that one thing. The personnel manager came out and said, "I want to thank you for your honesty but that lost you the job." I said, "Yeah, I reckon." I sensed that, as soon as I said that I don't like overtime then that was every bit of it. They didn't want me anymore. But I felt like I had to be honest and tell them that I don't like overtime but I do work it, I have worked a lot of it.

I forget now how it started but one day they called—the pastor didn't call me, somebody else from our local church called me—and they said, "Can you go up there and do some work for us?" I was just out of work from Harvester and looking for a job. "Well, yeah, I'll go up there and see what I can do." So I did that and then Father asked me to come back out about a month later and do some more electrical work so I did that. That's when he approached me and said, "How about working full-time?" So I thought, well, I'll take it on a temporary basis because the guy that he had before wasn't doing much, wasn't doing much of anything so he wanted to get rid of him anyway. Father was wanting somebody that could do everything and be sufficient without having to come and ask him every time, you know, "Should I do this or should I do that?"

One of the factors to taking the job was that my mother was getting up in age and she needed looking after and I thought, "Well, how will it be if I went out of town to work and I couldn't get there and she needed help?" So I decided, "Well, I'll just stay here." That was another thing that prompted me to just stay there. My wife was involved with her family. I'm an only child. So more and more I just stayed up there and I thought, "Well, this isn't that bad a job and I'm making expenses, so that's the main thing." I wasn't really in a hurry to run out and get my old salary back, getting more money.

I had to cut back monetary-wise but not a whole lot of difference. I mean, I just didn't have the money, the same money to spend. I wasn't making as much so I had to cut back but that was about all. That didn't stop me from doing things with them or whatever. As the children got older we still stayed close and that part didn't make a whole lot of difference there. We've always, not necessarily had a fixed budget, so we knew how much was coming in and we tried not to overspend. We tried to keep the spending down so that if I wasn't making enough then that's why I made that statement. If I wasn't making that much money then I tried to cut back. I remember back in the early '60s we were working down at L&N and wasn't making enough money. There was a point where we were perhaps going to—this was in the early '60s now—we were about to lose the house so I gave up smoking and drinking. Now, since then I've gone back to drinking a few beers but, and maybe a highball or two but not the smoking. I quit the smoking, I just quit completely. So back then we make adjustments to cut back on our spending.

I wasn't upset and I'm still not upset. I mean, these are just facts that I feel like are facts and you can't change it so what good is it going to do for me to get worried or upset about it. I guess I'm a firm believer of—I don't know who said it—something about, how did that go? Change the things that you can and accept the things that you can't and have the wisdom to know the difference. Or something like that. I've just sort of based my philosophy on that; if I can change something, I'll try to change it but if I can't, well, I can't. That's just the way I've always felt all my life. I just do the best that I can and whatever happens, happens.

Phil Nalley, International Harvester

It was pretty sad knowing all these people you had worked with all these years, you're not going to stay in touch with them. You're going to stay in touch with some. The seven of us that ran together, I see a couple of them now pretty regularly. But the others, one died, or one got shot; and one committed suicide; several moved off; one went to prison. I see a couple of them fairly regularly. One owns a carpet company and I work for Jewish Hospital and do maintenance and we need repairs and small jobs and I'll get him to do that.

Looking at the Louisville job market, it was nonexistent. Everybody was having problems and your interest rates on home loans were up to almost 15 percent and everyone had bought into these adjustable mortgage rate, ARMS. I've seen a lot of the people I worked with losing their houses because they couldn't keep them. You get to know these people, you've worked with people, you spend more time with people you work with than you do [with] your family. If indeed you develop a social circle within your workplace and you care about these people, it really makes you feel so bad. I did prepare and try to make it through this. But I saw the people that I liked, they were my friends, that didn't and they just lived like they always did. Then I saw a lot of divorces really quick because, there wasn't any money there, there wasn't any happiness, there wasn't any ability to continue on. Whether they would have stayed married anyway, I don't know. But you didn't know that there were any troubles on the home front until all of a sudden you hear someone is getting divorced. So yeah, it was pretty disturbing.

It was very, very stressful as far as my own home at that time. I became somewhat insistent that my ex-wife went to work. I really believe that it played in our divorce because she did not want to do it. She had not worked for nine years and I understood that she didn't want to but I finally looked at her one day and said, "We've got to do something because we're getting to where it's starting to fall apart."

Yeah, we can make the house payments, pay the utilities, and we can keep the kids in school, which they were in private Catholic school. But if they need shoes for basketball, we're kind of in a bind whether we can actually do that or not. I could not do any more and I felt that I was doing what I could at that time. I saw all these people with college educations that didn't have jobs. They were working in the same jobs that I was doing and the market here was flooded with laborers, people that were working at factories and so on and so forth as these companies moved out and laid people off. It was tough finding something. You always have that feeling, "Why did I fail?" You can say, "Well, it's really not your fault," but it still doesn't help that much.

I had always saved some money, and I made sure that what I was saving was going to be there when I got laid off, thinking that I had maybe a year of the sup-pay. I wasn't real worried. I still didn't want to spend that unless I had to. I looked at the savings as "I have to." It may be that I have to buy a TV because it's on sale at the price I want or I have to buy kids clothes because they're going to school. So there's a lot of reasons I have to do something. My car, I made sure that it was paid for. I did not take on any other bills. I don't believe in credit cards, but I think I did have a Bacon's or Penny's credit card—no telling what the balance was. I made sure they were paid off. I did things of that nature to prepare.

That's the way I was raised, you took care of yourself. You learned with all these other kids around that, yeah, you could ask your brother for help and your sister, but basically once you started working, you started taking care of yourself. I bought clothes when I was in high school. I paid for my last two years of tuition in 1970 which was $400.00, a lot of money, and supported my social life. So I knew that what I had to do was just find another job. And I did. I don't think I drank anymore or became any different than I ever was except, yeah, there was definitely those worrisome days. Working two jobs thereafter, that really changed.

I worked at my father-in-law's bar. He had done it for a lot of years and he was looking for any chance to not work. He wanted to come in the morning, and count the money, and set up for the next day, and make sure the kitchen was going, and then take off to go fishing or do the things that he had earned. So I worked with him. Then I went into a janitorial position at St. Ann's. My kids went to school there; I had helped with projects and done other things. I come from a large family and kids around me all the time so I got along with kids pretty good. So that's what helped me into that position. They already knew me. I'm a firm believer if you don't know someone, it's extremely hard.

You either have to be the cream of the crop, extremely lucky, or know someone. That normal person out there has a tough time.

The job paid surprisingly well. It had no benefits though. I think it was paying like about eight dollars an hour and it wasn't as much custodial work as it was a groundskeeper and maintenance. They used a lot of the high school kids every day to come in and to work off their tuition debt to DeSales High School or Bishop David or St. X. They could come in, and if you'd work there for ten hours a week you got twenty bucks or whatever knocked off of your tuition. So the kids would come over and I got to know them. I became their intramural basketball coach out there, that's one of the spin-offs of that. I took care of seven acres of grounds over at St. Ann's. I took care of the gym and learned to do some of the electrical and communications work. I learned a great deal from that job that helped me just around my own house, which was pretty valuable. I feel what I learned then I still use today. Even with the job at Jewish Hospital, I worked maintenance there and there are a lot of the things there that I learned that I still use.

After the custodial position at St. Ann's I took a job at a company called Konco. Konco was a manufacturer for the defense department. A friend of mine, he worked for the ammunition plant in Indiana, he told me of this place and he knew Harry Konky. So he said, "I'll give him your name and he'll hire you," which he did. Well, as time's going along, glasnost comes about and all of a sudden through no fault of my own I can see I'm going to lose another job. And my friend who's also my boss now, Bob Dooley, I'd been after him for a couple of years to let me come to work down there. They had developed a holding company within Jewish Hospital called J. H. Properties. We take care of all the properties of Jewish Hospital or Jewish Hospital Health Care Services, which is the outpatient care center down there, the doctor's office building. We've got a building out on 42 and the Watterson Expressway, one in Prospect, Westport Road—all over the place. So we've got all these buildings and we go to these areas and do the maintenance on them. I presently work at the outpatient care center and take care of the surgical suites and take care of the administrative floor. So I'm after Bob about going to work for them. I'm making about somewhere between nine and eleven bucks an hour and I'm experiencing the same thing I did at International Harvester, the unraveling of what I have tried to achieve over a three-year period. Bob keeps telling me, "No, you don't want to come to work for us. I can't pay you anything. It's $6.35 a hour to start." But he said, "There may be a future. We're looking at doing some things." Finally

I convinced him to hire me and I went to work for J. H. Properties or Jewish Hospital.

The job that I have right now, it's like I've got two days in one. My work day starts early, and then I get off so early and I've got, like if it doesn't get dark tonight until 9:30, from 2:30 to 9:30, seven hours of daylight. So I basically, I love it. Harvester shutting down was a setback and yes, it was a major, what I felt at that time, a major blow, but it has turned out for the good. I really enjoy this lifestyle. I get to use my hands at Jewish plus I get to use my mind. People ask me what my job is all the time because I deal with the doctors, the nurses, the administrative staff, the doctors' offices, their people, the vendors, the contractors, you name it, anybody that comes into the outpatient care center; in some way it seems like I end up dealing with them. My boss gives me a lot of leeway. He trusts my judgment. He allows me to think versus just follow. I'm glad now that it's happened. It's taken me since 1981 up to '91 or '92 to get back to the same income level I was. I've surpassed where I was in 1981. It has really turned out for the good.

Thomas Rhodes, International Harvester

[The plant closing] was very devastating even though I pretty much knew it was going to happen. At that point in time I had put about nineteen years with them with the intention of hopefully putting thirty in and getting my retirement and then possibly do something else in my life, because I would have only been forty-eight when I was eligible to retire. That had always been my goal.

So after being off for I think maybe six months I drew unemployment and just piddled around doing little odd jobs, painting for people and stuff and trying to make a decision what I wanted to do with my life, where I wanted to go. I didn't really have the educational background other than high school to go anywhere else or do anything different. At the time that they announced the plant closing, there had already been a lot of layoffs—not only at Harvester but all around town. What decent jobs were to be had were taken and there really was very little of anything left that paid anything. So it became pretty obvious to me that I was going to have to do something different or move or something. That really wasn't a realistic approach because my wife was working at Ford and had a good job, or at least what we thought was a good job. It turned out to be so, and she was making good money to a point where I had to be the one that had to do something and it had to be here. So I chose to go to real estate school.

I got involved in real estate through a friend who at one time had worked at Harvester; in fact, his daddy was in management there, a guy by the name of Dick Freeland. Dick had tried to talk me into it a few years prior to before he quit, he actually worked there. We worked in line next to each other. He had been working real estate himself buying and fooling around a little bit part-time prior to quitting and going into it full-time. He had tried to talk me into it then. Of course, I was young and dumb and didn't have any interest in doing anything more than what I did and that was basically just partying and having a good time and whatever I had to do to make the money to allow me to do that. But it was because of my acquaintance with Dick that I went to real estate school. I can't remember the exact terminology of it but they set up an office in our old credit union building over there for retraining supposedly, getting you into something else. It was tied into that Trade Readjustment Act, TRA. That was a process that the government had put together to try to help because there were a lot of plant closings beginning to happen around the country. It paid the 300 and something dollars for me to go to real estate school here and that's what I chose to do.

I think it was a wise decision. I didn't make great money but between the two of us what we made together we lived a pretty comfortable life-style. We didn't slow down too much, we didn't lose anything, and in fact we bought this house or it was being built while I was selling real estate before I got called back to Harvester. So I think we went on and progressed pretty well and did reasonably well for ourselves.

But a lot of people—and I don't mean it in any kind of deroga-tory manner—my brother being one, lost his home and everything he had. Some of them lost their wives, their family, their lives—people killed themselves—it was very devastating for a lot of people. It very easily could have been us too had we not had the, I guess, a whole lot of luck and some intelligence to where we were both working to start with in trying to achieve something. Because a lot of people I worked with were older people and their beliefs and their upbringings were still basically the wife was at home with the children and took care of the house. Some of [the wives] maybe worked a part-time job or some-thing, piddling around to make a little extra money. But most of them didn't have any interest in working in those days, they really didn't. Of course, it wasn't really the acceptable thing to do necessarily unless you were unmarried or something to that effect. As a consequence, I think, it was very devastating depending on what people had done. We made decent money at the point in time for the kind of work we were doing, no question about it. But unless you were very thrifty and very wise you never really made the kind of money that allowed you to make the investments and do the things that were smart. The people that really maybe weren't wealthy but had money were doing it. Some of the guys that acquired farms and some inheritance, there were a few guys—Mr. Miller's wife worked at Kroger as manager on Dixie Highway and he worked at Harvester and they had one child who was handicapped. But they worked hard, they were very serious and thrifty about what they did, they bought very few new cars, took very good care of what they had, and consequently when he retired twenty-something years ago, I mean, they've lived a very nice lifestyle. They built a new home. But that's just the way they lived and there were other people that did that too but for the most part people were not that thrifty.

In October of '87 I was recalled to, well, at that point it was Navistar. They had since changed the name. I rented an apartment [in Springfield, Ohio] and stayed up there from Monday to Friday and then came home on the weekends. We were most definitely not welcome there—they did not want us there. I say they, not only the people in the plant but the community as well and they made it pretty clear through articles in the paper every day about outsiders taking their jobs away from them and boaters. They called us boaters. It means somebody from out of town. They accused us of taking their jobs from them and in reality that's not the truth at all. During the plant closings there were new contracts negotiated, which allowed a master recall list, which guaranteed people, through seniority or service with the company, recall rights. That's how we got recalled was through this master recall list.

Like I said, it took until '87 when I was recalled. Now I could have been recalled prior to that, probably a year or so, if I had chosen Indianapolis. But primarily what they had been hiring for Indianapolis was people in the foundry up there and I had no interest in going to that. I had interest in going back, although at that point in time I never really thought that it was a realistic thing that was going to happen because they had closed so many plants. It had become quite obvious they were financially in bad shape and I never really thought it would happen to be honest with you. In fact, I was quite surprised when I got a call in my office one day and it was from Howard Etherton and he called and he said, "What are you doing?" I said, "I'm trying to sell real estate, man." I don't remember the exact conversation but something to that effect and he said, "Are you ready to go?" I said, "Go where?" He said, "To Springfield." I said, "What the hell am I going to go to Springfield for? What are you talking about?" He said, "The company's trying to get a hold of you to call you back to work." I said,

"You're kidding." I thought he was pulling my leg because after that many years, almost five years I had really just basically written it off and decided to go a different route with my life. I had forgotten all about it. But he was very serious.

I went up there and took my physical and filled out all my paperwork and went to work. I'm still not sure that it was a smart move but anyway I did it. You have to understand Springfield is in Clark County, Ohio, which encompasses about 145,000, or 150,000 people, basically a small town. You're looking at the whole community, the whole county being less than 200,000 people. Anyone that come in there from out of town basically was not wanted. They didn't want them. Especially coming into Harvester. Navistar it was at that point, which was without a doubt the largest and best employer in town. So we weren't welcome. The people of the so-called union up there fought us tooth and nail. I say the people, I mean the leadership of and the membership of [the national union]. They fought us and it wasn't because they didn't want us to come at all, it was that they didn't want us to have our seniority. You have to understand to start with, back to what we were talking about with the master recall list, what was negotiated was there had to be open jobs that were not filled by the working manpower— there had to be open jobs before anybody could be recalled. So we went in there on open jobs. Once we got there, at that point in time, then we were allowed to exercise our seniority. I was [friendly with some people] in the beginning but for the most part people were very bitter about us being there and they just quite simply didn't want to have nothing to do with you. There were a lot of cars that were damaged in the parking lot. There were people that literally got into fights in the plant. A whole lot of cussing and carrying on that went on. I mean, we were not wanted, we were definitely not and I never felt comfortable there.

I actually took a medical retirement [after about eight years]. During that period of time I had had a massive heart attack, had bypass surgery, had been off for a little over half of '94 from the heart surgery, six months, a little over six months, went back to work in January of '95 and worked until the last of April of '95 and had a light stroke and at that point's when I just quit.

I think [the closing affected me] in a lot of ways. To start with it's made me very bitter. I'm not as much today as I was probably. It changed a lot of the plans and things and I don't mean to be selfish or naive but it did change plans and things that I had tried to plan for my life. Not that everybody's plans always work out, I understand that. I think it affected my health. I'm sure it affected our relationship here at home—we're still married—but it did affect it, there's no way you can say it didn't, that'd be a damn lie to tell you any different. But I think in a lot of ways it taught me a lesson.

Kenny Rhodes, International Harvester

We had what we called sub-pay and that was 85 percent of what you grossed in a normal forty-hour week, that's counting your unemployment. We could draw that for as long as the money was there. In my case it was there for six months. I used that money for my training period to find another job and that's not really what it was set up for. It was basically set up to help you get along but I used it for what I was going to do. I felt like I had a six-month window that I had to decide what I was going to do with my life and go from there. It was a pretty rough time. We ended up losing our home and basically everything we had, but I guess that goes with the territory.

We did okay for that first six months but after that things were shaky because the trucking industry that I got into, you were not paid on the hour, you were paid on the load, the miles. You had to go out there and hunt to get it and I guess I just probably really wasn't as good at it as I would like to have been or should have been. It was new to me. I was probably feeling a little dejected over the fact that I lost a good job. We had built a home in 1980 because everything at that time, at least what we were told, looked very good for our future. I had planned on working at least thirty years and I was eighteen when I went there, so I would have retired certainly after I was forty-eight years old. We had a home, we had just built it ourselves and, of course, my wife still had her job but it's a two-income family and take one major income out and all of a sudden things weren't as rosy as they should have been.

[I left Harvester] probably late '82 I'm thinking because my father passed away in February of '83 and I bought a semitruck it seems like in August or September of '83. It would have been a little longer than my six months' money that I got, some sub-pay, but it was shortly thereafter. I went out with a guy who had a truck and he kind of taught me the ropes a little bit. Then I went to work with a company that probably would hire anybody and learned the hard way on some things. Then I decided that I'd get out there and try to buy my own or finance my own.

I drove different type trucks: I drove tri-axle dump trucks hauling rock and asphalt and helped build the Jefferson Freeway so that was something I did I guess. I helped build UPS when they first started with pads and stuff for the airplanes; I drove a semitruck. The dump truck was a good business other than the fact that it was seasonal. Once the weather turned bad about Thanksgiving you're done till pretty much the spring. Semitrucks, it was just a touch-and-go deal. But I did that for a while and then in '85, I had my heart attack and that took me out for about seven months. Then a friend of mine, Kelly Stamper that I worked at Harvester with, had bought his own truck and he hired me as a codriver to run the West Coast with him. We worked for an out-fit called Victory Freight Ways, which is now gone. In the meantime when I was running with Kelly, I got to be friends with the operations manager at Victory. I finally got to talking to him and I told him I'd like to make a career move, and he took me in the office and hired me as an equipment manager. I just run time on all the tractors and trail-ers in the fleet, where they were at, who was doing what, and where. Then I went into dispatch. After I went into dispatch, I kind of had a falling out with some of the dispatchers that I worked with because I didn't like the idea of them lying to the drivers about freight and loads and where they were going and such. We had a big confrontation at one of the meetings and he gave me the opportunity to go into the safety department.

My next venture from there, I went to work for a company called Sodrel Truck Lines in the free enterprise system, which is a motor coach company. Mike Sodrel, the owner, hired me as director of operations and I was basically overseeing all the operational ends of the trucking here in Clarksville. Then about two years later he made me vice president of the company and that gave me the nice job of overseeing everything we did, which was a traumatic change of life for me being that I worked in a factory for many years. But I enjoyed that. I was the first person outside of family members to be on the board of directors and I thought that was quite an accomplishment. I enjoyed that for about seven years and then I left there and took up a job at National Distributors, which is another trucking com-pany. I only stayed six months and then I got a chance to go back to Navistar in Indianapolis and I went back there. The main reason I did go back was because I knew health-wise it was starting to go down and I knew I wouldn't have as much retirement from the other companies that I would have there. So I went back to Indianapolis and worked, I guess technically I was there two years—I probably worked a year and a half of it—and I had three heart attacks in between that time. On the last go-around, my doctor told me that he wouldn't give me no more opportunities to work. And he retired me. So now I sit home.

[When I went to Indianapolis, the people there] weren't happy. I think they had what they called SOS and I'm not really sure what SOS stood for—save our shop, save our seniority—I don't know what the phrase was, but I think the people that went back a couple of years before me probably had the hardest time. They didn't like the out-of-towners taking their jobs and taking their work from them. They felt like they were stealing from them. But the truth is they agreed, when they took their vote on the contract that anybody that lost a job, if a job opened up somewhere else in the system that they would have the opportunity to go to it if they had seniority to get there. So we really weren't doing anything to hurt anyone. I had a couple of confrontations with some of their people. As a matter of fact, one of them was president of that local. It's like I told him, I said, "We can either work together at this or we can continue to fight and go backwards. The bottom line is going to be that I've got seniority enough to do a job and if it gets bad enough to where they have layoffs, you're going to get laid off before I am. Now, we can either work together and make it work or we can fight each other and watch this company go down the tubes like it did in Louisville. Pretty simple."

I had a very good job at Sodrel's, I had a very good job at National Distributors. I learned a lot. I found out that there were things that I never thought I could do that I could do. I never was really good in school, and I found out that I could make things happen and do some business things that I really didn't think I could do. I got a chance to meet a lot of interesting people and I got to negotiate part of a union contract, I enjoyed that. I had a lot of responsibility and I enjoyed that actually, just to kind of put your foot in the fire and see how the other side does it. It's easy to sit up there and point fingers and say, "These manager people are the bad guys." But when you get over and you realize the responsibility they go through—once I got on the other side and seen there's a lot of give and take running a business. And, of course, the bottom line is the bottom line, just making a profit. You try to make your people happy and pay them a fair wage and good benefits.

[The closing] changed my perspective about trying to plan for your future. I don't feel like I did a very good job of that. I guess it was really a reality check to realize that what you think is going to be there for you for a long period of time obviously can be taken away in a short period of time. I think it's probably made me a better person. It's obviously made me more aware of people and things. I think it's been a very good learning experience. I wouldn't recommend it for everybody, but I'm better for it. I don't begrudge International Harvester or anything else for it. What is, is. I really don't begrudge the union for the most part. I think ignorance was bliss back in those days, it was always us against them and I think that was a poor mentality for people to have. I think if you sit down sometimes and analyze exactly what's going on and especially if you do you probably do understand why they do what they do. You can understand and even justify it sometimes. Some of it depends on the way you personally want to take it because if you're just a "against the world" type person then you're probably going to die a very unhappy person. I did that, I went through all those emotions and I'm not interested in doing that anymore. That's history. But I believe by changing the jobs I changed too and probably having the heart attack, it was a very eye-opening experience.

When Harvester went under and our sup-pay run out I really wasn't making it as a truck driver. Obviously I was obligated for the home that we built and automobiles and such and it was basically a two-paycheck family and we cut out more than half of mine so we were unable to take care of our responsibilities. So I lost a home and an automobile and ended up taking bankruptcy to be honest with you. So that was pretty depressing to be seeing what we had. I guess that's one of those "woe is me" for the way things are. But again, I believe that was a good learning experience. I believe there was a reason for all these things to happen and I don't think it was necessarily poor management or poor judgment maybe on my part but there was probably a reason for it to happen. Maybe I was going the wrong direction or something. Probably I was going the wrong course, not maybe!

Howard Etherton, International Harvester

When they closed the plant, the last guy left the Harvester plant on April 9, 1985. At that time the company and the union offered me a job that I had helped negotiate in '84 for what we called a benefit rep. I stayed here in Louisville on that job, which my seniority went on and my benefits and everything and my job was to assist anybody that needed help on their insurance problems, their pension problems. I set up my office at the Local 1336 union hall and I was there forty hours a week to assist or help any of the people that had been laid off. Now, it was quite a time before some of these people got recalled. Well, we had a lot of them that lost seniority and didn't get to go. A lot of these people went from 1982 until like '92 or '93 before they got called, so they had as much as ten, eleven, twelve years of some real hard times really. A lot of them lost their homes, their automobiles. We even had a few people commit suicide. Several divorces, a lot of divorces. I was kind of like a minister and a union official both.

[The closing] didn't affect my life because I continued right on here working. The portion that affected me was that even now I see guys that lost everything they had and they still are out there working for a whole lot less pay than what they was making ten years ago when the plant closed. That portion bothers me a lot. Most of your skilled trade people, especially the machinists and the electricians, most of them have found jobs comparable to the ones they had at Harvester. It's just the common people that didn't have any skilled trade or really a lot of education, they're the ones that really suffered from the plant closing. Maybe some of them didn't have but eight or nine years and that eight or nine years is completely wasted because they get nothing for it ever. They didn't have enough to get any benefits any time down the road from the Harvester plant.

I'd get calls at home all within the night, I have ever since I've been laid off, "What's my chances of getting called to Harvester? When you think they're going to call some more up to Springfield?" I mean, people are desperate and that's the kind of calls you get. "Well, my wife left me." You wouldn't believe some of the things that they would talk about or call me about. That portion of it was depressing.

We was making $18, $19, $20 an hour. So there just wasn't no jobs out there that these people could go to and a lot of them had big house payments and a car payment. They had good insurance, free insurance for their families. It was just a whole lot more than some of them could take. Some of them kind of went off the deep end. I don't think there was a lot of people that committed suicide but there was some of our people that did. The divorce rate went real high. In other words, even the people that got called to other jobs up to the plants, they'd come in and tell me that, "Well, the wife wouldn't go up there and she didn't want to live down here by herself," and he'd come home on the weekends so she filed for divorce. Then, of course, when they went in the plant up there they had to take a job that was open. That was what the master recall language said. Then once they get there, they had just like Springfield, they had people that was working up there with eight or ten years' seniority and once they got in that plant then a job come open, they had twenty-one, twenty-two, twenty-three years' seniority. A lot of our people up there had twenty-eight years' seniority, and when they went in the plant and when a job come open, these older guys, our guys, they called us boat people, called our people boat people and they resented it.

Danny Mann, Johnson Controls

I put back money. I was one of the individuals who saw this thing coming and I started socking it back. I can't afford to hunt like I did. I miss that. That's probably the biggest thing I miss, being able to go to Colorado and New Mexico. I've been to Colorado like five times and would go up on horseback, up in the high country, stay in tents. I'm on the horse from about four o'clock in the morning until about eight o'clock at night. I miss that, riding the Rockies. That's my relief. I had so much pressure on me all the time because I had to come up with an answer; I had to have the answer all the time. I quit stopping [at the bar] across the street because I quit drinking. Before when I was running around and all that stuff back before I got married I'd stop across the street with the guys. We'd all go across to the liquor store and we'd all sit over there and drink beer. It wasn't nothing to go through ten bucks, every night. Then I started taking those ten bucks every night and putting it in the credit union, and I said, "I'm going to Colorado." I went out there on a vacation and I said I was going back out there going hunting. And those hunts were like 2,500, between 2,500 and 3,000 dollars, to go on a guided hunt. But that's what I wanted to do so I sacrificed one for the other and I extremely enjoyed that. That's where I'm at. My dad and my uncle and my brothers went, well, some of my brothers went and my best friend went and we was all sitting around the fire one night and I said, "This is where I'm at. This is me." My uncle says, "Danny, the only thing bad about this was you was born a hundred years too late."

I didn't know what I wanted to do just after the plant closed so I just looked. I didn't want to go back into—not unless I had to—an industrial environment. That place had beat me to death. Jim Studley who was plant manager, he told me, "Well, do you know what you're going to do now?" It was just Jim and I off the record, and I said, "Well, I don't know for sure. But I can tell you what I'm not going to do." And he said, "What?" I said, "I'm not going to build no damn batteries no more. Last Friday was the last battery I'm going to run." I thought about going back to school, but I thought Danny, you're too old and you're too ignorant. I went through _____, that was a farce.[2] You talk about a joke. I bet you I spent two full tanks of gas going down there. I told them, I said, "You social workers are a joke." They asked me if I'd take a job for seven dollars an hour. "No! No!" I said, "Hell, I can go to Krogers and bag groceries for seven dollars an hour." It was like, "Well, we're doing the best we can." Those people are a joke. Why the government pays those people to do those things I'll never know. They act like that you're some-body from Sesame Street. Don't talk down to me. I might not have your education but I understand the English language quite fluently. Don't talk down to me.

Then they got in all this retraining stuff, all these people jumped in and I said, "Wait a minute folks, wait a minute before you jump, before you jump and do this stuff. Find out how long it's going to last. If you jump into a two-year program if they're only going to pay for six months, what are you going to do? Where's the money coming from? Think about what your moves are here. You're playing chess here with your life." [They were sending people to] Kentucky Tech. I said, "That's a two-year program. What happens when your unemployment runs out, what are you going to do? You spent all this time trying to retrain and doing school work, you haven't looked for a job; now what are you going to do?" I wanted to retrain in heating and air; everything is going to HVC. It's all heating and air and I wanted to do that. You get certified in HVC and that's eighteen bucks an hour. Everybody's got closed windows now. But I couldn't go to school, maintain my home without losing. I've got to rob from Peter to pay Paul and I refuse to go into debt.

But, I couldn't find anything that paid anything, nothing near what I was making. I had a job offer to go back driving a truck, semi again, but I wasn't going to do that. Been there, done that. I have a small child—I'm divorced—and I'd never get to see him so I went to work for Kroger maintenance. They told me they'd take me on, if I worked so many weeks, I'd go to full-time. Well that didn't pan out either. It was like they put a hold on taking you full-time. "We like what you're doing and you can stay and we're going to keep your hours going, but we can't give you benefits, can't take you full-time." Well, that's time for me to go someplace else. None of the guys wanted me to quit in the maintenance shop over there; they said, "Man, you're our entertainment!" I said, "Well, I got to go, you know, if you talk to Larry, make him give me full-time I'll stay, but I don't think that's going to happen."

So then, I went to work at _____ and that place, that was a trip.[3] It was nonunion and the foreman, everybody bowed and stooped. Well, I don't bow and stoop to anybody. I do my job. I don't kiss butt, I do my job. Whatever you tell me to do, unless it's going to endanger my life, I don't care, I'll do it. But I'm not coming over and washing your car after work. I'm not going to play buddy-buddy to a guy because he's the boss and make him think I like him if I don't. I'm straight up and straightforward and so I wasn't going to get anywhere. So I saw an ad in the paper for a maintenance tech at Home of the Innocents. So I went there. And I've been there ever since.

I do everything from boiler systems to leaky faucets. It's running three different buildings and the convalescent center. I don't like to go in and do the same thing, I like challenging things. I can make things work, I can fix things, and make them work. I like that pretty well. I mean, I don't like the pay but I think that will grow a little bit in time. I've never worked in an environment like this. I've always worked in a place where they're cracking the whip, move, move, move. I've never done this type of work before as far as building maintenance and all that. It's very technical in some of the equipment that they have down there. When I got my check the vice president down there, he had signed my check, "Thanks a lot for all your hard work." I thought it was a joke. I was playing around with the girls in the offices up there and I thought it was a joke. So I went back in there. I said, "Y'all will have to get up earlier than that to get me." And they said, "What?" I handed the check across the desk there, and I said, "You'll have to get up earlier than that to get one on me. Try again." They looked at me and they said, "That's Tom's signature. That's his writing." I said, "I'm impressed." That's a first for me.

So, it's different and I like it. Sometimes it's a little too much. I feel like I can't get all I want accomplished but they tell me things take time. But it's been good. I'm good at fixing things. I'm good at building things. It's pretty much set on my own schedule, and my own pace. "How long does it take to fix it Danny?" "I don't know; it will probably take thirty minutes." I enjoy this a whole lot more than I did production work. I told him, I said, "Being union rep again, I wouldn't take that job for a million bucks." Maybe a million bucks, I mean, I'll do anything if the price is right. But I want to go to work, I want to do my thing and come home. I found out that there's more in life than money. Although I'd like to make more it doesn't interest me like it did. There for a long time I was consumed with the buck. Between Johnson Controls and making money on the side, that's about all I did. I thought money was the key to happiness. I found out that it didn't matter how much money I had. I might have more things but I wasn't going to be any happier. So I decided to stop and smell the roses some.

Still, I don't have time to do what I have now. I called my buddy the other day, well, last night and he said, "Well, is Didi still alive?"—that's my horse—I said, "It's been about three weeks since I got to see her. Is she still alive? Still kicking?" I don't know. It seems like now I don't have near as much time as I did but when I worked at Johnson

Controls. I sure do miss living three miles from work though. I don't miss the work. I don't miss that part. I miss the money. Just like I told Dibiagio that day, I said, "Jim, it's like this: I have no allegiance to Johnson Controls because Johnson Controls has no allegiance to me."

Ron Phillips, Johnson Controls

A lot of people had this thing—we put in all this time for this company and this is what they're doing to us. It never did bother me that much because they never treated me wrong. They treated me good; they paid me good. I never got hard feelings against the company. Besides that, when they did shut down, I had a chance to transfer, which I did. I went to North Carolina for about three months to another plant. I just didn't like it. My family and friends were here. That plant down there was different, the way they operated. The people were different. So I just turned in my resignation and came back home. It was getting to where I was going to have to sell my home and stay there. I had to make a decision. So I said, "Well, I quit," and I come back home.

When they started talking about closing the plant, I said, "Well, that's not good but maybe it is. Maybe it's time to do something else. I still got quite a few years before I can even retire. My pension's locked in. When I get fifty-five, I can get whatever I got coming to me." So all that's there but then it's sort of a relief. You're waiting—two more weeks, one more week—getting out of here. To me it was getting to be a relief. This was going to be over with and I'm going to do something else, which at this time I'm doing something I enjoy better than I ever did there.

I'm a service technician working on RVs, campers, trailers, motor homes. I really like it. My dad has always bought campers. He's always had trailers and the guy he bought it from—they were talking one day and he was saying he'd have to hire somebody to work there. He needed somebody to work. Dad told him, "I know somebody could do it." So that's how it came about. I really enjoy it. Last year I did odd jobs in the summer, then I started at this place over in Bluegrass. I didn't like it but I was just more or less doing things to—I still got to have an income coming in. Finally, I said I'll do something to get me through the winter, which was that job out in Bluegrass Industrial Park, and this here came up. I just came to it and I've been there ever since. I really like what I'm doing now. I like it better than Johnson Controls. It may not pay as good, the benefits may not be as good, but I enjoy it. I like going in. I like doing the work. I deal with a lot of people now. Before, I didn't. The customers I deal with—sometimes it's good. Sometimes they got problems. Sometimes they're mad. But most of the time, they leave happy. I go to their homes. I go to different lakes. Friday I was up in Indiana, Potoka Lake—I was up there all day. Just little odds and ends: brackets on shelves, a doorstop was broke. Just little stuff. But these people's got their trailers parked. They got them set up and they're living in them, like a summer home. It's easier for us to go there and fix it than it is for them to load it up and bring it all the way back here.

It's constant because in the winter we do estimate jobs, which is say somebody messes one up and it needs to be gone through. My boss told me, "You don't have to worry about it." He said the year before it got slow and they had to let somebody go for two or three weeks here or there. He says the way the outlook is, I'll be busy the whole time. I go in at nine in the morning. I don't have to get up early. All them years at Johnson Controls, I had to get up at four o'clock, be there at six, work till two-thirty. Now, I start at nine and I get off at six in the evening, so I don't have to go to bed early and I don't have to get up early. I get home at six and there's still daylight. I like the hours. I like the work really well and the people I work with. There's only about ten of us out there. Everybody gets along fine.

I see very few people now that I worked with [at Johnson Controls]. Every now and then I'll run into them. Sometimes one or two of them will come over and we'll talk awhile. They'll say what they're doing and I'll say what I'm doing. They're doing okay but they're doing eight to nine dollar an hour jobs. They're getting by. I know there's been two or three of them died. One of them a heart attack. They keep saying that's stress related from losing their job. They tell you that before this ever happened. They'll come in and say, "Some of you is going to have health problems; some of you is going to get divorced." Cause that's part of it; that goes with it. So here we got this in our head before we're even gone. But these agencies come in and tell you this is what happens. You just hope it's not you it happens to. Some of them went to truck-driving school. Some of them went back to school more or less to get an education. A lot of them there probably didn't even have high school educations so I'd say a lot of them did that.

Any more you've got to have some college to get into it. Throughout the years we had a lot of courses; we got computer training. Usually everything that came along, I tried to take more or less to better myself, better my job, the knowledge of my job. I was in the Navy for quite awhile back there in '69 to '71. I had a lot of training in there and I guess that's what got me into the mechanical type field that I stayed with, machine and knowing how to run it, how to fix it. Even when I worked at Johnson Controls, I did a lot of work on the side. I'd work on cars: tune ups, brake jobs. Always did something—plumbing; I did electrical. But a lot of this knowledge I gained through work. I could go out and wire somebody's garage or basement or just about wire a house and I could do plumbing. But that's just something I learned throughout the years and now it all came together. I do a lot of this where I work now. I do it all. It's anything and everything. I might do upholstery work. Somebody's got a couch that's tore, might get in there and sew it—or the carpet is bad, replace the carpet. I never really did all that—maybe a little here and a little there, but now I do it sort of like a living. It's interesting. It's different every day. I go in there tomorrow hard telling what I've got to do. Put on air conditioners, hitch work. It's just different every day. Johnson Controls, every day I knew what I was going to do: I was going to make plates. If it wasn't for the money, it probably wouldn't have been a good job and it probably would have been very monotonous. But, the money and the benefits—take home 800 to 900 dollars a week, that makes that lousy job look better. It makes working in lead look a lot better.

[The closing] wasn't that stressful on me. I was pretty well set here. My home was probably three-quarters paid for. I guess the only thing that changed was I had five weeks vacation and now I have none. I was making 50,000 dollars plus a year and now I probably make twenty some-thousand dollars a year, up to 30,000, in that area. So I took quite a cut in pay. My lifestyle has changed. I can't go like I used to. I'm not getting the vacations I used to. Before, I had it scheduled where I'd just about get a week every month. With the way the three-day week-ends worked out, I could add a couple of days and get five. Now I don't have that. Here, all I got to do is say, "Jim, I need to take a few days off." He'll say, "Here, take a motor home. Go take a vacation." That's how he is. He said, "I'll fill it up with gas. You go on." That's how they are. I can get a trailer anytime I want it. Don't cost me a penny.

But at first it was hard. Most of it was, I can't do what I used to do. I can't go, I can't buy. I don't know if it was stressful. A lot of people had all these stressful things happen to them. Mine wasn't like that. I made that decision. I could have went on and worked down there in North Carolina. It was my decision: No, I don't want to work here no more. At first it wasn't good cause I wasn't doing that great and I wasn't making that kind of money. When I quit down there, that more or less said, no, you can't draw unemployment. You resigned. I didn't get that option so I had to go from that into finding work. At that time I was probably taking anything that come along, but a lot of it was construction work, which I like. I was outside and I was building decks and fences and stuff like that. I made pretty good money in it plus I still had money left from severance pay. So I was taking that and putting a little severance pay money with it and paying my bills and whatever. It wasn't that bad. I know a lot of them's had harder times. They probably lost their homes and everything else. There was some of them had just bought a home or just had kids. My kids were—Tony is twenty-two now so he was twenty or twenty-one and my oldest boy, he's twenty-five now so he was twenty-three or twenty-four then. They're more or less on their own. It's like Tony, he works at Toyota and Brad, my oldest son, works at DJ, Incorporated and they both do good. So it's not like I had that. And I was divorced well before this ever took place. That wasn't no cause of none of that. I wasn't that bad. A lot of them still got young kids and they probably got full mortgages to look forward to where I don't.

I like what I'm doing. I don't think I'd ever go back into [factory work] again. It was punch the clock, you got to do this, you're expected to run so much. That's the only job I ever had. I never had to look for a job before. When I got out of service, I wasn't really looking. Somebody said, "You want a job?" I said, "Well, maybe I need to work. I don't know." I was twenty-one so I went to work. So I've never had to look for a job until after that was over. Now you fill out applications and you got interviews and interviews. You got to fill out resumes. Back then, you didn't do that. You wanted a job, you go in and say, "You all hiring? Okay. I'll start to work tomorrow." That was it. Now you got to put in your resume.

But, you got to look at us. Some of the places I went to, at my age they are not going to hire you. [I went to the Johnson Controls plant out in Shelbyville]. They made seats for Toyota down in Georgetown. Being the same company, I said, "Maybe I have an advantage here. I've worked for this company and it's close to home. I can drive out there in forty minutes." So I sent in my resume, what I'd done at this other Johnson Controls plant for years, my service record, all my education I had. I said, "I should have a good chance getting on here." I never even got a response. I never got a call. I called them and said, "Was my application ever considered for employment?" "We can't give out that information." So I never heard a word from them. I tried Toyota, Ford out here—they're just not hiring no people in that age group. They say, "Well he's only got ten years left. He won't benefit us." So, that's what I look at and a lot of people my age does. You get in your forties, you might as well—they're not going to hire you. They want somebody they can get twenty-five or thirty years out of.

I just have less money. Even though I'm making less now, I'm probably happier now making less. I don't know if it was a stressful job. You had production requirements—we got to have this many batteries. Ford's got to have this many, Toyota's got to have this many, Nissan's got to have this many. We're behind. You need to get your production up. You got a lot of that. Now I might have, "These people would like to go camping this weekend, see if you can get their trailer fixed." But there's no pressure there.

I guess the only thing that's affected my life is I don't have the benefits I had, and I don't know if I'll ever have a pension plan out here. They're talking about a 401K or something which I guess would be okay, but we're going to have to contribute to it. It used to be every other year or so, I'd buy a new vehicle. I don't see that coming up in the near future. If I can maintain what I got, I'll be happy. I got a decent home, I got a decent vehicle, I got a boat. I can do the things that I want to do. I can't do it as often. I can't take a week off here and a week off there. I can't go to the beach like I did before. I can make do with what I got. That's probably the only part of my life that's changed. I got the same friends I used to. Nothing's really changed in that way. I didn't lose no friends over not having that job. Probably I got more support from my friends and family—if you need anything or if you see you can't make it, you let us know. I got a lot of that. Even my neighbors they say, I know that you had this job and I know you don't have that job no more. We don't want you to have to sell and move because you're a good neighbor and a good friend so if something comes up where you need help, you let us know. I've been told that by all my neighbors back here. I may not be a person that you're looking for to interview. You might be looking for somebody that's had more stressful things happen or maybe lost something or maybe caused a divorce or something like that. None of that's affected me cause I'm done past that stressful part. Everything I do, I'm easy. I don't want none of that hassle and stress in my life. You need some of the ones where, "I hate Johnson Controls cause of what they done to me." Some of them, it may ruin their lives.

But I don't have no hard feelings [about the closing]. I'm not going to be a disgruntled postal worker. It's over and I like what I'm doing. I'm sort of glad it happened; it gave me something else to do. Some people, it don't affect them like that. Some people, it's going to cause that kind of problems. I just don't want to be around that. I was looking at the positive things that could happen out of this instead of the negative like a lot of them were doing. A lot of them, they were down on them. I left a few weeks before they really shut down because they told me in Winston-Salem, "We'd like to have you down here," so I wasn't there the final day. I sort of got out and I was sort of glad to get out because it was gloomy; the atmosphere was bad. Morale was bad. People knew day by day it was getting closer and closer. Some were getting jobs other places—you're allowed to go any time. You've got your severance pay. A few was going to different places; they found something. Some of them went to Philip Morris and just anything that came along. But the majority of them was still there. They had found nothing. They kept thinking, "Maybe they're going to change their mind." That wasn't going to happen.

Roy Puckett, Johnson Controls

I didn't know what I was going to do at my age. I was forty-six at the time and I thought, "Well, I don't know what I'll do now," because most companies say they don't discriminate against you for age but once you get in your forties they're not going to hire you if they can hire younger people. So, I went down and signed up with the unemployment, and the computer kicks out so many people that they want you to go back to school. They knew that I had the carpal tunnel at the time, so I was going to have to change my style of work. So, in the meantime I was upgrading at Kentucky Tech and trying to decide what I was really going to go into—something that wouldn't involve my hands so much. At that time I had got a call from the president of local 862 over at the Ford plant, he was president of UAW over there, and he asked me if I'd be interested in a maintenance job with them and I said, "Oh, I would imagine." That's probably the greatest thing that ever happened in my life because I just didn't know what I was going to do. So I went to work there and I really enjoy that. It's probably the best job I've ever had in my life. You don't punch no time clocks and you work for union people. I think the union people are just the greatest people in the world. They just treat people nice because they know what it's like to work for a company. And we've got our own little union and it's just a great place to work. There's no words to describe it.

I do the maintenance on the building, on the Union Hall. I keep all the filters changed on the air conditioning, do all the grass cutting, clean the front offices, and that's about it. I started there in October [1996] so on October 14 I'll have a year. My unemployment had run out three days earlier.

Most of the people found jobs, they really did and I was so glad of that. I think basically everybody that wanted a job found one. And some of them were pretty good jobs. As a matter of fact, we were really surprised and I think one thing that helped in the economy—it just happened to be getting good about the time that we closed; unemployment was going down and I think that's really all that helped us. Because a lot of companies, normally they wouldn't hire you when you get up to our age but they were in such a short supply of young people, that they had to take about anyone that they could get. Now, a lot of them didn't go back to making what they were making. Some of them were making twenty dollars an hour there and you just don't find those kind of jobs. A lot of them went to factories. We had several that went to Coharts in Louisville and we had several that went to a place out in Jefferson County where they worked on those box cars, trains. And we had several that went on to school up at Kentucky Tech and got some additional training. If we wanted to go to Kentucky Tech the state would have paid for some of that retraining and that's why we were trying to get the NAFTA benefits. If you kind of get that all to coincide you can draw unemployment, extended unemployment while you're doing that. But they denied us that. It was a point to where my unemployment had ran out. I was either going to have to drop out of school to get a job or get a job and stay in school too, so it was at that point.

I was still real worried. Actually, I tell you, we just didn't know what we was going to do. As a matter of fact, my wife and I had already decided we were going to sell the house and just move to the country and just scratch out a living somewhere. Of course, we weren't in debt real bad. We just started getting out of debt when the rumors started floating about three years before we ever closed. So, we were kind of looking at things and thought, well, we better get our financial house in order, because tomorrow's not promised to anybody and we could be one of those plants. We didn't think at the time we would be but you always get the thought in the back of your mind that it could be.

By that time we had already bought us a small farm down in the country and we were kind of working on that. Actually we were trying to make us a retirement home. So then once that happened, why we kind of had to put our plans on hold there and we said, "Well, we've got to see what's going to happen now." We eventually thought we may have to move down there and maybe go to work. We started saving money immediately and started trying to get out of debt as fast as we could. We just tightened our belt. We spent a lot of money because, me and her together, we made pretty good money together and so we just decided we was going to quit our spending and just started paying off some of those bills. We got those bills down to where we could survive on her paycheck while I was drawing unemployment and going to school at that time at Kentucky Tech.

It messed up my retirement plans. I think I would have come out much better with a retirement plan had I been able to stay there and finish out all my years. And financially, I was making more money there than I am now, which eventually I'll get up to where I was. I guess that was the biggest thing, was the pension thing. When you go to work somewhere you think you're going to be there all your life and anymore that's not true.

Buddy Pugh, Johnson Controls

When you go to work somewhere else for ten dollars less an hour it's hard. That's the flow of the country. The country, the wages are going down instead of going up. The cost of living is still going up, not as great as it was but still going up. But I've been pretty lucky—I've been able to work ever since I've been out of there. I've been lucky about getting jobs.

I worked three different places. I worked at one of those places twice. The plant closed on March 4 of [1996] and my last day of work was March 1, which was on a Friday. I went to work at Publisher's Printing at Shepherdsville doing what I'm doing right now. The pay wasn't all that great, it's still not, but it's on its way up. But then I heard about this other job so I went to see about this other job and I quit Publisher's and went to work at this other place. I worked there a week and in the meantime I had started my communications with another place in Bardstown—it was a factory—and they had called me to come to work. So after a week I told—the place that I worked it was a construction company—and I told them, I said, "I've done factory work all my life and I need to go try this." And they said, "Well, if it don't work out for you, come back and see us." So, I went up there and worked for six weeks. I didn't particularly care for it so I went back and saw the construction company or called them up, and they said, "Come on back and work on Monday if you want to." That was on a Sunday that I called them. I said, "No, I want give a week's notice." So I gave them a week's notice and I quit and I went back to work with the construction company. I worked there about eight months. I worked at doing office work and I didn't like that very well. So I went back to Publisher's. Well, all three of these places that I worked, they told me that if I ever needed another job to come back and see them. So I went back to Publisher's and asked them for a job. They said come on to work the following Monday and I've been there for the last five months. It's a good job, it's a good job. Publisher's is the place, if you work there a long period of years you'll make real good money but you start out [with] low pay.

I'm working as, I guess you might say a carpenter or whatever. It's more or less carpentry work. It's carpentry, painting, building cabinets, whatever. Whatever pertains to that type work. Drywalling. Kind of a construction type thing. Maintaining the plant I guess is what it would be more than anything else. I'm going to stay there for a while. I'm planning on it. If something real good would come along I would probably consider it but I really like what I'm doing, I really like what I'm doing. They're probably as good a people to work around, my fellow workers, as I've ever worked with anywhere.

When I worked at Johnson Controls, I liked it in a way but what really made me stay with Johnson Controls was the money. The money was real good. But this here is probably the best job that I've ever had. The only thing is it's not the best-paying job I've ever had. It's no secret, I tell my boss that. When you work at some place almost thirty-two years, you kind of get in a routine and you miss the people and you miss the work and you miss the money and you miss the benefits. When it's something that you counted on retiring there all your life and they up and kick you in the face and kick you out, it don't make nobody happy. I figured I've got to buckle down and make it until I get ready to retire. I said, "I've got ten more years until I'm sixty-two years old or when"—that was when the plant closed—I said, "I've got ten more years to work and possibly thirteen more years to work until I'm sixty-five. I've just got to start all over again." And that's basically what we've done.

The only thing is it's a lot harder to make it now on six or seven dollars an hour than it was twenty years ago. You kind of got to watch your ps and qs. You don't buy your furniture for your house and do remodeling and such as this that you did do. You don't take vacations because you don't have any vacations to go on and you don't have any money to go on vacations and such as that. That's how it changed for us. I had five weeks' vacation where I was at and I had thirteen holidays and I've gone now for two years without any vacations. Where I work at now we get six holidays a year. After you're there a year you get six vacation days and four personal days. The day-to-day spending [has changed]. Nothing big. We may have built another house by now. I like it here all right but we'd like to have [a new one]. You're afraid to spend money. When you go from 47,000 dollars a year down to 15,000 a year, it's hard. You don't have the money to spend. When you bring your paycheck home on Thursday and when you clear not hardly half as much as you did when you were working and that half don't buy nothing. It does something to your ego—that's what it does. It just does something to me. Here I am expecting to retire from a place at fifty-something years old. Where am I going to get a job at that I can make a decent living at it?

And then sometimes I think it was a blessing because of the health hazardous work that I was in, it was a blessing to get out. I knew I could get a job because I'd already had a job but the thing is I couldn't make the decent living that I had been making, that's what it amounted to.

It's going to make me work until I'm sixty-five years old instead of sixty-two. It's going to make my retirement pay a whole lot less because if I'd worked another ten years for Johnson Controls I'd have been able to draw some more retirement, a bigger retirement. Now I'm paying forty dollars a week for insurance so it has a big effect on you. You got to lower your standard of living, that's what it amounts to. It wouldn't be so bad if you could go out and get another paying job of good pay like I was making but you can't do that.

I don't have no really harsh feelings. I just don't like the way they kicked people out. I just get mad on payday. I have a lot of resentment. I have a lot of resentment to 'em for taking my living away from me. Especially when I worked hard, and everybody else worked hard too and it wasn't really from a lack of work, it was something else, some of their money-saving schemes or techniques or something was the reason they moved. I have a lot of resentment.

Marilyn Reed, Johnson Controls

By the time they closed I was glad they were closing because I don't know how much longer I would have been able to work there doing that type of work. It was really physical work and I would come home and I couldn't hardly lift my legs up I was so tired. I was relieved almost when they closed. I know that's not fair but that's me. I wouldn't have been happier on any other jobs that were available there because they were all hard. They had added so much to everyone's job that there weren't any jobs that were, I don't want to say easy to do but that just didn't wear you out or give you carpal tunnel or hurt your back. So I don't know how much longer I would have been able to work there as far as my physical condition—I was getting to where my hands were going numb and things like that. So, I thought this is my chance to do some of the things that I've wanted to do that I wouldn't be doing if they had stayed open because I would have stayed there until I was either handicapped or retired maybe at fifty-five. So, that got me to where I could go to school and learn computers, to work with computers. I was going for the basic things, and to get out of that environment.

I'm a payroll administrator. Same thing I started out, in payroll. But there's a lot more, a lot different. I've got to be a personnel manager and put people on payroll and all kinds of stuff. Some days I hate it and then some days I just figure, well, it's an office job. I would like it more if I got to use my computer skills that I went to school for because I'm not using my computer skills. I'm using my accounting skills, but they're supposed to be going to go online with the company that does our checks. See, I do all the time distribution and put it on sheets and then I send it to Louisville Tabulating and then they print out the checks and quarterly reports and things and then I take my figures off of that. So we're supposed to go online with them so I'll have to get a new computer, so I think I'll like it better then.

Like I said, I was more or less relieved when they closed because I hated the job that I was doing so much. It was to the point when I would go in there I would almost be in tears knowing I had to go in to work and I didn't know how many more years I would do that. So I was more or less relieved to get out of there. Losing that money was a big thing, because you get used to buying what you wanted and paying cash for things and that's taken away from you. But it balances out to have the peace of mind that you're not in tears before you even leave the house knowing that you have to go to that job. I know there's so many people are bitter and blaming the company and saying, "Well, they didn't do anything for me, they didn't do this." The way I feel about it is they paid me decent wages. I worked there for so many years and they weren't any different than any other big business. They're out to make money just like everybody else. That's the name of the game, to make money. They said, "Well, they cut our throats, they stabbed us in the back." But I didn't look at it that way. I don't have any harsh feelings toward the company for closing down. I don't feel like they dumped me or whatever. I think they could have offered us more. Like my unemployment ran out in July and I still had six more months of school to go so I think that could have been extended. But I don't know if you blame the company for that or the state for that. It seems like you can't do anything unless you make a minimum wage job. Then they said, "Well, we'll pay your way to go to school but then we won't give you any money to live on."

[The closing] was really bad. It was sad. It was real sad. Because people were there because they need a job, and they have children, and they have expenses. And it was really good money, and you tend to live on what you make. If you're making good money, you're going to buy you a nice car, nice home. You're going to buy your kids this and that. You're used to living like that, and then it's all going to be taken away from you. There's not that good-paying jobs out there like that for the people. Because as far as myself and Bob [Reed, also a Johnson Controls employee], we're older and we don't have any children to raise. We didn't have any bills, and things like that so we knew that we could make it on a lot less income. But there were people that just didn't know what they were going to do. And they didn't have any experience. A lot of them didn't have high school educations. Some of the people could not even read and write. One guy, he was about forty-five to fifty years old, he would ask me to read things for him. I didn't know that he couldn't read for a while. Then he'd ask me to fill the work order out for him. He could sign his name and stuff, but he really couldn't read very well at all. So, that's the people—that's the working-class American, more or less. So they were like, "What am I going to do?" So, it was very depressing, very sad.

There wasn't any [jobs available in the local market] I don't think. That's why they said we could only draw unemployment for six months. They said unemployment was down and there were plenty of jobs out there. But, they were like six and seven dollar an hour jobs. You go from eighteen dollars an hour—I wasn't making that, but people out there were making that. Bobby was making that—I was making like sixteen—that's still good money. You go from that to six or seven dollars an hour, which is what they're making where I work. The groundskeepers or the maintenance people and housekeepers—they're making seven, seven-fifty an hour. That's what's mostly out there on the job market now, and they think that's good money. Even when I went to school they gave me this printout that had the average salaries for the Louisville area for the type of work I was getting into, and it was like $15-19,000 a year.

I had twenty years in there. I had twenty years, the pay was good, and the benefits were good, and then retirement. You think you're going to be there until you retire. Because if I would have stayed there for five more years I would think—the way Bobby and I were saving money with our incomes—I could have retired at fifty-five. That was like five more years from now. I could have retired from there and got me a job in an office working doing something I enjoyed, and not been just wore out.

Mike Reid, Johnson Controls

I'm sure it has affected me. Financially. I'm not making quite the money I was. I was making a lot of money and saving a lot of money. I'm not saving any money now and I'm spending more. I miss the four weeks paid vacation. But I haven't suffered any financial hardship over it because my wife has a good job, she makes good money. Not huge money but she makes good money, enough to keep us going and we don't do without anything.

It's got to have affected me more than I realize. I realize now that I'm going back to school that I'm not going to lay out of school as long as I did before. It's been twenty years since I've been in school and now, knowing what I know now, I think I'll probably always keep my foot in the school door. Even when I get done with this program I'm still going to try to take night classes and pick up on something else. You just don't realize when you stay out that long how long it takes you to pop back up. Especially with some of the classes I had to take, the math classes, algebra. I didn't like it that much when I was in high school and I hated it even more when I had to take it. You go twenty years without taking it, without going to school and then jump right into it, it was a big adjustment there. And probably being dependent. I'm an independent person anyway, always feel like I've been independent and now I'm kind of depending on my wife. But she doesn't seem to mind. She's been supporting me the whole time, going to school. She won't let me drop out—if I wanted to she wouldn't let me.

As a matter of fact, I feel better. That's the lingering effect—I feel better that I'm gone. I don't miss that place at all, no. I'd be lying if I said I missed that place—I don't miss it at all. I was relieved when they closed it down. Probably because of all the stress and pressure they put on you to do production.

There were a lot of them probably that got hurt over it because they were so close, the ones that were over—between fifty and fifty-five—if they were fifty-five and over they got, I think, full retirement. I believe that was the cut-off, fifty-five and over got full retirement. But the ones that were between fifty and fifty-five, if you're fifty years old or fifty-two whatever, they didn't get anything. They won't get anything until they turn sixty-two or sixty-five. Now, see those people got hurt because they're going to have to go find a job and they've got say, twelve years to go. The only kind of job that somebody fifty years old—they're not going to get the primo jobs that pay big bucks. So there's a lot of them that got hurt pretty good over it and if it'd been open another five or six years they could have been fairly well set. It did hurt a lot of them. I figured I was one of them young guns, I'm thirty-nine, so I can start over.

Bob Reed, Johnson Controls

We had a lot of older people working there but the majority of us were in the age like forty-five to fifty where you cannot take an early retirement, you have to go out there and get another job. You're just right on the cusp of missing that thing. Some were fifty-two, fifty-three, right there and they had to get a job elsewhere making probably a third of what they were making there, no benefits. A lot of people that I saw down there at Job Link were saying, "Golly, I don't know what to do. What can we do?" And "I could kick myself in the rear end for not going back to school years ago." But you make that kind of money, you make good money, you got good benefits, that's the only thing that kept me there. I figure I had to work there. I don't have to do that no more, thank God, and now I've got choices. We've all got choices and we need to take them instead of being forced to do something.

I never lived beyond my means. A lot of people in there bought new houses two years before the plant shut down and I know they're probably up in debt to their ears and they have to worry about paying that kind of thing off. It changes your whole lifestyle, it changes your whole way of living, it changes your whole viewpoint on a lot of different things. A lot of people say you shouldn't hold resentment for the plant being closed down and I said, "I do and I don't. I do because I put twenty-three and a half years in that plant. I put forth a 100 percent every week and every day, made this company what it is today, me and the rest of us, and this is the only kind of thing that they give you to justify all this hard work and everything": a severance package that Uncle Sam takes 50 percent out of and here you are. You can sign a release form holding nobody responsible for what happens to you later in life. I mean, come on. Yet they're still going, they've got all these plants operable, they got their hands into every kind of thing there is, technology and plastics and everything and here we are out there without anything. So what good did it do other than we learned not to work in another factory again. Me for one. I ran into a gentleman today and he said, "Don't you feel better that you're out of there? Less pressure, don't you feel better physically?" And I said, "Yeah." The lead dust that we were exposed to for the first years that we were there without all these things that put in, there's no telling what it could have done to a lot of people. I mean, so much lead dust and dirt and chemicals and stuff and gosh, until the union started negotiating on health and safety and really pushed the issue forward. Thank God the union did that or else we'd all be probably in a nursing home somewhere or probably in a six-foot box or something.

I'm always thinking I've got to provide my share of the responsibility, bring in money to pay for bills and stuff. I went in every day and made the money, had good benefits. But now it's a challenge far exceeding anything I've ever done in my whole life. I mean, we've been through scary situations before where, let's say trying for new jobs when we were out of high school, things like that. I got laid off a couple of times at work and things got pretty rough when I first started working there. I got laid off nine months and I didn't have an income coming in, there wasn't any jobs out there, that was scary but I ended up going back to work, we survived. But this is a new type of pressure that a lot of people are facing now and it's really hard to cope with. You look at yourself and you say, "Can I do this? Am I capable of doing that?" You're sort of challenging yourself, but sometimes you don't think you're good enough to do this. It's really a mind-boggling experience. You say, "Golly, I don't know if I can handle this. Am I smart enough to do this?" Your intelligence really plays a lot to do with this especially if you take these tests when you go out to find another job. You say, "Gosh, it's been a long time since I've been out of school. I feel like a real, complete dummy. I don't know anything except for working on machinery all these years." You feel incompetent, you don't feel like you can compete or you don't feel like you can live up to your own expectations. That's what it boils down to right there.

I feel like I'm getting a lot more depressed than I was before because I'm not attaining what I want to get. I was really getting depressed at work because of the conditions. I was really getting fed up but now it's a different kind of depression. I've got these dreams and I really want to do things but I'm not doing the action, the getting yourself up and doing things. It's a scary thing and I'm just not comfortable with it. I know I'm not satisfied where I'm working now but I know I'm good at it or I know I can do it, fulfill the responsibilities and all, but I'm lacking something. I feel depressed for that, that I haven't fulfilled any of my dreams.

[The lifestyle change] was almost like turning a water [faucet] from cold to hot or hot to cold, that drastic. The major thing I miss is the income and the benefits. The benefits mostly. We had six months' benefits covered after the plant closed and you could draw unemployment up to six months. You didn't have to worry about the pressure of finding a job immediately. We went out looking. I went to every job fair there was. I was trying to find a job that was suitable. There were a lot of jobs for five, six dollars an hour but when you're making nineteen, twenty dollars an hour it's kind of hard. A lot of people look at you and you think, you made this kind of money, you don't want this kind of job. I went to two or three interviews and they looked at me and they said, "Well, you're making nineteen, twenty dollars an hour, you're not going to be settling for this." I said, "Well, I've lost my job. I don't have a job." They said, "Well, we'll consider you," and you never did get a call back. It scares them because they think you're going to quit on them in a heartbeat because you're not content with that kind of money. So it changes your whole, I mean, you feel like you're in a lost world. You were stuck in a routine and so your life was structured. Now, the bottom falls out and you've got to go out there and try to start all over again at forty-five years old.

Now, you've got one strike against you for age. Of course, now there are laws and everything about discrimination about age and all that stuff, but that's bull because it still happens every day. You're thinking, well, you go back to school, by the time you get a bachelor's degree, that's four years out of my life and you're going to work full-time somewhere else. Well, what kind of job you going to work for four years? Are you going to be able to pay for your college education? I mean your mind is just constantly swimming all the time. When you're in the plant and the plant's about ready to close, "Well, oh, yeah, I'll go out there and get a job," and this and that but it's not going to happen. Reality sets in once you're out there and looking and find out, you don't have the education, you don't have the training, you don't have anything, you're lost. And you're dumb for not trying to do it before. Now, you feel like you're insufficient. You don't feel like you're capable of doing anything other than running machinery all your life and maybe that's all you're going to be. A factory job or assembly-line job is all I'm going to get for seven dollars an hour, seven-fifty.

No, I don't want that. Now that everything is taken away from you, it's a chance to live again at forty-seven, forty-eight years old now, almost getting to fifty years old. A lot of people are scared. It scares you, it really does. It scares me about half to death. You're caught in the middle. You've got your dreams out there about pursuing what you really want to do but then common sense tells you that you've got to be able to make a living. You pay for your bills daily, you pay for this, pay for that. In order to do that you've got to have a job every day. If you relinquish that job, every day you're putting your sibling or your spouse, more pressure on them to fulfill their half or to support the family. I don't want to put pressure on her. But, if my mind is gone, if I'm totally depressed about not accomplishing what I want to accomplish and have to work in a construction company busting my rear end every day like a twenty-one-year-old and I'm almost fifty, I can't do it like I used to do it. Why should I have to do that? I want to do what I want to do, doggone it.

CHAPTER 5

"There's No Such Thing as Job Security Anymore"

Throughout the interviews, the former employees of International Harvester and Johnson Controls shared stories about what their experiences have meant to them. They examined what they learned from their work in the factories and from the closings of their plants and insisted on sharing these lessons with the interviewers and the absent but imagined larger audience. A number of dominant and interconnected themes about lessons learned weave through their narratives. The first and most prevailing was a loss of trust. These narrators have lost trust in the government, their companies, workplaces in general, and management. In particular, employees from International Harvester and Johnson Controls have come to see companies as unstable and managers and executives as out for themselves. These narrators repeatedly stressed that the people in charge of these companies care only for themselves and their bottom lines—not for their employees.

The narrators also stressed a second theme centered on negative projections for the U.S. economy. In particular, these interviewees warn that living standards are declining and the income gap is widening. In short, the rich are getting richer, and the poor are getting poorer. Moreover, they believe that NAFTA caused a host of economic problems; in particular the closing of many manufacturing facilities. Indeed, NAFTA and the movement of plants abroad, especially to Mexico, fueled much of the distrust for the government and management. In a related vein, these workers expressed concern that other countries are taking away U.S. jobs, building their factories here, and being allowed to own too much in the United States, all with dire consequences for American society.

The mistrust of management and the government and feeling that executives care only for their profits, combined with the perceived turmoil in the U.S. economy caused mainly by the movement of plants outside national boundaries, led these narrators to conclude that unlike their fathers and others of the preceding generation, for them and their children there was no job security anymore. Now, because companies and governments cannot be trusted, they must look out for themselves and not rely on anyone else, not even fellow workers or their unions.

Some of the narrators moved past that pessimistic conclusion and reached for more positive lessons for themselves, their children, and workers in general. In this they repeated the pattern seen in other chapters of striving to end on a note of optimism that belies a sense of victimhood. They insist they would not want their own sons or daughters to enter manufacturing work and urge them to get an education instead. Indeed, several former employees see education and retraining as critically important paths to personal advancement. Finally, and perhaps most interesting, a common thread in these narratives is that despite lowered income from job loss, some former employees maintain that they would not go back to factory work, least of all to Harvester or Johnson Controls. Their new jobs offer opportunities that their previous ones did not, and many have reconciled the changes into their lives in positive ways. In short, the lesson they seek to emphasize is that despite some acknowledged decline in their financial situation, they are more fulfilled doing other forms of work.

Below former International Harvester and Johnson Controls employees describe how they view work, companies, and the government, and the lessons they learned from the closings of their plants.

Charlie Noyes, Johnson Controls

As far as what I learned from it, you don't want to put too much trust in anybody outside of yourself. I guess that's a cynical attitude, isn't it? I went along life's way, partly because of these failures, that you had dang well better trust yourself because there's nobody out there you can trust. It just doesn't work that way in this world. Cynical as that may sound, don't never put all your trust in a union, a company, your banker, or anyone else. You better take command, of what you have, and do the best you can with it. Even if it isn't much, it's something, you know. Anything is better than nothing. With the way the situation has gone today, I can't see where anything a fellow can do is going to make him much better off. It looks to me like, and I've seen this transpire over a period of years, and it's only my judgment, my personal opinion, but if you look at the situation today, you're in now what's called a global economy. We now have to "compete against everybody in the world." For years and years, all my lifetime, I probably had the best of everything in the way of a living, really even coming from the meagerest of beginnings. Throughout my lifetime, it developed; this country developed into a position where I could rise from absolutely nothing. I'm not a man of wealth, but I am comfortable. I don't think our children, my children and my grandchildren, are going to be so blessed. I think the best time, you've already seen.

Primarily, if you want to get into that, if you consider the number of people in this world and their living standards, and you can testify to that because you just came from a very poor family, there is not enough resources on the face of this earth to bring everybody up to our standards. If we are going to let the business community engage us in a "global economy," there's only one resolution. They are going to lower the living standards down to meet perhaps a rising Third World economy. There's no option. Let's assume that you, myself, and my wife are the three prominent business people in this country. We all have numerous factories, we employ numerous people, and at the beginning, they are all paid a good wage. We're manufacturing products. We're making something from raw materials. We're selling it with value added, and that's where our profit comes from, okay? So now me and you and Dolores control all the economy in the country. And all of a sudden I look around and I see people in Mexico that I can hire for thirty-five cents an hour, so I look around and opt for that. I close down my plants, which is a third of the country's production, lay off a third of the country's workers, build myself a plant in Mexico and hire people at a much cheaper wage, thinking all the time that, "Boy, I'm going to sell this stuff and look how I'm going to increase my bottom line." Never realizing I've already put one-third of the country out of work; those people can no longer buy what I'm producing. And my wife looks around and says, "Well that dude—look at the money he's making." So she closes her factory down and she goes down there or to Honduras or El Salvador or Taiwan or wherever. It's offshore. Now there's two-thirds of the people in this country that are no longer able to buy anything. They're starving to death. Where in the hell does that leave this country? There's no way that that's going to work.

Like I say, I'm an old man. I hope I've gained a little wisdom over time, but you're seeing it on the streets today. It's already out there. These people out there selling dope, there's a whole lot of them would rather have a job like I had in my lifetime, I can tell you that. They're taking and making money any way they can. Now, it's only going to get worse. As we go downhill, there's no way for that situation to improve. It's only going to get worse. At some point, at the rate that the wealth is being siphoned off at the top and the division grows greater between the haves and the have-nots, at some point in time, the people in this country are no longer going to stand for that, all right? Before they starve to death, they'll take up arms and take what they have to have. And that's exactly the reason why you got the politicians up there in Washington trying to take the arms away from everybody right now. An unarmed person puts up very little resistance. An armed person can take care of himself. And they know that. There isn't a doubt in my mind that they know that. So what you got to do is slip around and, "Well, we got this big problem, we'll have to take away some of your liberties here, we'll take away some there." All these killings that have been brought about lately, we're going to have to take and disarm you people. We can't afford to have all these guns—a gun never killed anybody. It's the person behind the gun that did the killing. Alright, I'm very adamant about that. I bought my first gun when I was fourteen years old.

Howard Etherton, International Harvester

The unions fought that [free trade with Mexico] to the end. I don't know how familiar you are with that. That started under the Reagan administration and then Bush picked it up and went on with it. And then, of course, when Clinton run for president the unions all backed Clinton. I'd say that 90 percent of the unions, maybe 95, supported Clinton, and Clinton was against that free trade with Mexico. But once he got in there all of a sudden he changed and shifted that way. I think it's a bad thing. I think it's going to get worse. And exactly these things that I've been talking about, a lot of them refer to that. Just like the Harvester plant taking concessions. It's either that or they're going to shut down and go to Mexico, which they did. They're building a plant in Mexico right now, the Harvester people are. And then what they'll do, a little later on, they'll say, "Now, you take some more concessions or we're going to go back down there in that plant in Mexico with all of our work." And they got a right to do that. They can run away from them as long as it's out of the United States, they can run away from them.

It's not just the jobs that we're losing. . . . The jobs that's going to Mexico ain't the ones that's hurting us. It's the jobs that the people right here in this country are threatening to take to Mexico [that are] bringing the standards down and the prices and the hourly rates down in this country here. Harvester people, in 1979, like I said, there was

43,000 UAW people; now there's 8,500. Five years from now, them 8,500, most of them will be gone, and the people that took their place will be making half of what they make now. Because they give them the right, either they do it or they're going to close it down and go to Mexico to cut the wages in practically half. And the benefits. The companies today, before the free trade with Mexico, the NAFTA thing, the company wouldn't think about coming into Harvester and telling you they was going to cut your pensions or they was going to cut your benefits. But they'll tell you now, "We're going to do it or we're going to take them to Mexico." Mexico ain't big enough to take every job out of the United States and put in there, but they've got enough hold, the companies do, to bring all the good-paying jobs down to a level to where the rich man gets richer and the poor man gets poorer.

I resent the Japanese coming over here and being able to build an automobile up here in Georgetown, Kentucky, for five or six dollars an hour less than what our people makes out here in the Ford plant. I resent that. I don't think they ought to have a right to do that. But, you know, this is a free country and, of course, we've tried to organize. UAW's been in that [Georgetown] plant trying to organize it forever since it's been there, and we ain't got it organized yet. See, the thing of it is, they bring them up there and they give good jobs. They want to hire a 100 people tomorrow, and they'll get 20,000 applications because they pay $13.00, $14.00, $15.00 an hour, which is good. But the only reason why they pay that is because they don't want to go union, see. So, you know, the free trade that we're talking about, it's kind of lopsided, it's one-sided, I think.

I don't even know that I would vote for Clinton again for that reason [free trade with Mexico]. I know that I did this last time because I didn't feel like I had much choice with what else was running but if somebody else would run..... Of course, again, you can probably tell I'm a Democrat. It would be hard for me to vote a Republican ticket, but I'm strictly against the NAFTA deal. And, you know, Clinton could have stopped that. I know there was a lot of pressure on him from different people. And they're even wanting now to expand that... FastTrack [extension of NAFTA to Central and South America].

Another thing I resent, I resent the Japanese, you know, coming over here building all their vehicles, or selling them. I resent them a whole lot. I think they've took a lot of jobs away from our people to bring the Japanese cars into this country. We got probably three times as much tax or tariff or whatever they call it to take one of our automobiles over to Japan and sell it than what they can over here. I know I had the figures on it one time. And I get a newsletter from the UAW all the time, and it was like a Crown Victoria Ford over here costs us $20,000, it would cost you $50,000 in Japan, see. That much difference in it—import tax. You know, Canada's probably got the best thing on that—Canada, if you don't make the vehicle in Canada, you don't sell them in Canada. You know, Harvester's got a truck plant in Canada; if they didn't we couldn't sell a truck in Canada. So maybe that's what this country ought to do. If they're not made here, you don't sell them here.

Danny Mann, Johnson Controls

I think that companies are very unstable. The dang, the durn Japanese are buying everything. I mean, if people would just sit back and look, the Japanese own the United States. They own property, they own businesses, they own controlling shares—it's scary.

Ron Phillips, Johnson Controls

I've always worked. I'm always going to work until I can't or say I've had enough, I quit. But it [the closing] hasn't had no effect on how I think about work. Like I said, I probably won't go back to Johnson Controls because what I'm doing now—I see there's another way of making a living that's a whole lot more enjoyable, a whole lot more easier, and I guess the environment is better. At that time when I was there, that's all I knew. I never done anything else. I got out of high school, I went in the service, I got out, and I worked there ever since. So that's really all I knew. I never had to look for a job, never had no reason to. I made good money and had good benefits.

Companies are going to do what they got to do to pay their shareholders because that's what it's all about for them. Money's what it's about. When they can make the same product in Mexico for $5 a unit instead of $21 unit, that's what they're going to do. That's more money for them. And all companies are the same. They move in and out every day and more here in the last few years than ever before. That Ford plant in Michigan shutting down—well, the article was in the paper yesterday; this [Ford] this plant down here is offering these people $10,000 to come down here and work for forty-five days in Louisville. Automobile workers up there. They stay two years, they get another $20,000; they stay over four years, they get the full $45,000. That's a good incentive for them people if they can come down here and relocate. To me, that's good that Ford is doing that, at least they are offering their employees something different. See, I didn't get no high offer like that. Mine was on my own. I had to make my own move and my own decision. I didn't get them incentives.

But all big companies like that—I don't guess they have to be big, look at all the insurance companies been coming and going here out of Louisville. Some other city gives a big incentive—"You come here for a year you won't pay no taxes or something, we'll build you a building"—They're going to take it. That's why Toyota's in Georgetown. They get free—five or ten years, they don't have to pay no taxes. So, whatever incentives are offered these companies, that's what they're going to take. They're looking at the dollar. I'm at a small place now. One guy owns the company, there's eight or nine of us, and we're all happy. We got a problem, we talk to him. His door's open any time. If he's not there, we call him at home.

I'm not anti-big company cause I worked for one for years but I know what they're doing, which everybody else does, too, I'm sure if you read the paper or anything. Down in Mexico, they said that big road down there, it's like an interstate. There's Ford, General Motors, Johnson Controls, GE—they all got plants down there. It's like all Fords they're made right down there in Mexico. Stamped right on them. I do wiring and brake controls on these trucks for these trailers, to pull them. They've got Mexico wrote all over them. They used to be made up here. They're going to the cheap labor. They don't have the environmental controls down there they got up here. I don't think I'd want to live in that area where the pollution is cause they don't have no restrictions or controls on all that. Ford—up here, between the truck plant and the other truck plant out here, they can only do so much. They're only allowed to put in so many hours—that's why they don't have three shifts. They only got two because any more hours they're putting out more pollution than what is allowed. But down there, there's no restrictions. They can run twenty-four hours a day, seven days a week.

Roy Puckett, Johnson Controls

They kind of drilled that into us at the unemployment office and through Kentucky Tech that you can look to change jobs five or six times in your lifetime now. They talk like from the '90s forward, where used to be you could go to work and you'd be working for the same employer for thirty years.

I don't feel as secure as I did at Johnson Controls. I know Ford's a big company but Ford could decide tomorrow, "We're going to close down and move." As a matter of fact they're in the process of closing a plant now in Ohio. They've got some employees that are going to transfer down here. So, there's no such thing as job security anymore. Each contract, that's all everybody would talk about, "Give me some job security," but really there's no such thing. We had in our contract that the company couldn't close the plant until they gave us six months' notice, and actually that helped us keep the plant open longer because the company would have to do that to comply with the law.

You keep that thought in the back of your mind, you know it can happen to you, no matter where you're working at. Right now I should feel real secure because I work with UAW and along with their union so I shouldn't have any worry but still it's in the back of my mind, even though Ford's big they could close the plant down. But I think really, as you get older you get a little more secure because you know you're closer to retirement age. But the ones that were really hurt, in my opinion, are the guys that have been there fifteen, twenty years. The ones that have been there like say, twenty-eight and thirty, they may feel a little more secure because they knew they had a little bit of retirement to fall back on. At least anybody who was fifty-five could.

My own belief is that the United States ought to get a law to where companies can't just move to Mexico with the high-paying jobs. The average worker in Johnson Controls made about nineteen dollars an hour and they went down to Mexico and paid those people like six, seven dollars a day. And, you take Bill Clinton, and all the unions are behind Clinton a 100 percent, but that's the one area that I feel that he really let unions down when he pushed NAFTA.

UAW does a lot of research. They predicted, once it [NAFTA] passed that we were going to see a lot of jobs leave the United States, especially the high-paying jobs. I'm sure Clinton's got this idea on his mind, we create all these low-paying jobs and it puts a lot of people to work. But, people's having a hard time. I don't know how these young people survive on minimum wage. A lot of them has to work two and three jobs. It's tougher than I always had it. I was fortunate to get that job over there and fortunate to be making what I'm making now. I just wished I could have got everybody in our plant the job like I had or a job at Ford or somewhere.

I tell you I wouldn't never want to go through another one—plant closing. I didn't think it would ever happen to me. I thought back when I started to work, when you started to work for one company you'd be there till you retired or died. Once we got into Job Link they told us that you'll change careers five to seven times in your lifetime now with the way the economy, the way it is. That just kind of blew my mind. So, really when you stop and think about it there's no such thing as job security. I don't care if you work at Ford or where, they can close those big plants as well as they can the small ones.

Buddy Pugh, Johnson Controls

There ain't nothing they [the union] can do. When the government opened it up for worldwide [such as with NAFTA] instead of keeping it at home, that's what it amounts to. I don't see why the government had to lower our standard of living down with the rest of the world. I never have understood that, and that's exactly what they're doing. It's not a fly-by-night thing. It's in the long-range plans of theirs, but I don't know why we should lower our standard of living. That weakens our country, and that's exactly what they did. Now, I'm not blaming Clinton and I'm not blaming—there's Clinton, Bush, and Reagan, all three was in on it. They started, brought it up when Reagan was in.

I don't have no trust whatsoever, and I don't want no politicians around me. I don't have no use for politicians whatsoever. Because to my way of thinking, they ain't nothing but a damn big bunch of crooks that's out to screw the working man. And they've done it.

I think Johnson Controls is going to do anything they can make a dollar out of. Like I said a while ago, the worker is just a number instead of a person. I don't think they have any feelings whatsoever toward the worker. I really don't. I think it's been that way from day one. But now, they gave some good benefits, and they gave some good things to the workers, but I think that was because that [the workers] fought for them and got them—I don't think they gave them out of the goodness of their heart.

I think they're [Johnson Controls] a rotten outfit. I'll tell you exactly what I think about them. They told us what they were going to do, or they didn't tell us but we had heard it from other sources in 1974 when they bought it what they would do. They would bleed it dry and get rid of it. But since it took really eighteen years after they took over full custody, you might say of it, we thought they might keep it open, but they didn't. And right now I'll tell you exactly what I think of it. I went to WalMart, they make WalMart batteries here, and I was talking to a man in there—they had a line of batteries that he was marking in there—and I asked him, I said, "Who makes them?" And he said, "I think Johnson Controls makes them." I said, "You want me to tell you about what I think about them? I wouldn't buy one of them if it was the last battery on earth." That's exactly what I think because if they can't tell me who manufactures that battery anymore I won't buy it. I would buy Exide, one of our competitors when we worked there.

Kenny Rhodes, International Harvester

It's a free-for-all. There's no question in our country, the way it is today, I don't believe there's any real major security anywhere. When I was young, eighteen, nineteen, twenty years old—could go to a Ford or a Harvester or a General Electric or Henryville Machine Company or Globe Union, American Standard, any of those type of places, at least before then, where they do their thirty, thirty-five, forty years and retire. And it's just not that way. I guess some of them still are but when you start getting into Ford's two-tier system, bringing in younger people to work part-time it's rather obvious their intentions are to basically weed out the very undesirable or possibly the older people, put them out on medical or whatever and then fill in with younger people. I guess it's just kind of the rule of the jungle, it appears.

Being what the economy is today for a lot of people, I can really appreciate what they're going through as far as hard times. I hate to sound so repetitive but it [losing his job in the closing] built character. [With my wife's] job the way it is, we're survivors and we'll figure out a way to get through it. We trust God and we believe He'll work with us and we'll work with Him and somewhere in between there will be a happy medium. It's all just a short period of time no matter what you do anyway. Like that old saying, "You can't take it with you," and that's really true. If you put so much emphasis on materialistic things I think you're in for a lot worse hurt if something does happen. I feel like I've got a comfortable home, it's decorated moderately well, furnishings are nice, we're happy, they've got their health, I've got what I've got. Obviously I eat well and I don't feel like that I have anything to be down about really. I do hate to see our country go the way it's going, but obviously there's nothing I can do about it other than vote. And I do vote.

I believe they're selling our sovereignty with NAFTA and GATT. I believe the Federal Reserve has got entirely too much authority on what we do and don't do. What I mean by that obviously is they control the purse strings. I mean, from everything I can read and find out they're probably more powerful than the executive branch of the government, so I would say that's pretty much in control. I think someday we'll probably reap what we've permitted to happen. I don't mean it like revolutionary or anything.... I've always voted. Years ago I was probably a Democrat; I'm probably a lot more conservative now than I've ever been in the past and that doesn't mean necessarily that I think that all Democrats are liberals and all Republicans are God-fearing, Christian conservatives because I know that's not really a true statement either. There's conservatives and liberals in both parties. But I do think I appreciate some of the views, if you will, of what conservative is versus some of the liberal views. But to say that I think they're all perfect and the others are all wrong, no, not at all.

There's no sense in going on about politics. I mean, I guess it's just an opinion like anything else. When I say I hope to see our country do good, I would like to see our country have, be furnishing jobs for people like my son so he could get a good-paying job with decent benefits. I'd like to see our debt down in our country. I don't know how well our country would function without debt but still, I mean, that's kind of what you hear on television. I hate to see us lose the rights and stuff that we've all grown to enjoy through our history. But that needs to be part of the plan too, it all goes together. I don't know, I'm no authority.

I think time's run out. I think eventually here shortly the Lord will be back, and I know that we'll all be eating and drinking and sleeping and doing what we do. But as I think you can tell me that things are getting worse. I mean, things are not better as a whole. I mean, unemployment may be down but is that because people are working or is that because people aren't on the call no more? People are working maybe in some cases but they're not making what they made. There's definitely a division I would think in economics as far as the rich and the poor. I don't begrudge people that go out and make a great living and don't think they ought to be taxed to death, but I think there's a tremendous division. I think drugs and a lot of this plays a major part into it too, because people are, they're searching. I mean I think people are, even if they're doing well, are still searching because there's not a fulfillment there.

Bob Reed, Johnson Controls

If I have anything to tell people about working in production in a plant or any kind of manufacturing, please, while you're working get an education. Go out and get some kind of either an education or some kind of job experience somewhere, a different way of life or a different thing because nothing is secure in this world. It'll fall right out from underneath you in a heartbeat. Don't think for one minute that you're going to be secure in that job for the rest of your life because it's not going to happen. We had a professor from University of Louisville to come down to Job Search or whatever it was, and he said that most people in their lifetime will be changing their jobs five or six times. He said, "There's nothing secure in this world and there never will be." And there might not be any retirement or anything else when we come to it. He said, "You'll be working until you're sixty-five or seventy. There's no such thing as a permanent job in the plant." And we all thought that when we first got the job. "Oh, we're going to be here till we retire." Thank God there was a bunch of people in that plant that did get to retire. When they shut the plant down, they were old enough to retire.

It's like I say, if there's any opportunity to change your lifestyle about what you want to do or your field of expertise or whatever you're pursuing, now's the time to do it because the company gave you that option, in a sense. It wasn't any option, they just shut the plant down—this is the way it's going to be—so actually they forced us to do what we probably should have been doing a long time ago and change professions or get away from that environment. There was a major cost involved—your livelihood and your income but that can always be straightened out. I don't need the income I needed before because we paid the house off and things like that but you learn to live with a lot less and be more comfortable with it. The only thing money and monetary things are going to bring is sometimes a lot of pain and suffering because you got to worry about keeping it, and you got to worry about making the bills and worry about losing this and that. If you're comfortable with what you've got, what the heck? You don't need to get out there and live far beyond your means.

But you get in that mentality of making a living, and you don't want to try anything else. You're comfortable with the situation and the environment you're in, and you don't pursue any other interests. It's just because you think you're going to retire there, and you don't want to rock the boat. I just say, you've got to forget that attitude and get yourself retrained, retrained and retaught. They need to teach kids in school that right now. I think the American dream is probably, if it was there, it's gone now, as far as the white picket fence and the two cars in the driveway and all that kind of stuff. It's a whole different way of thinking now, and it's not that it's not achievable but it's not the same.

Never think that anything is secure. Never rely on somebody else to pay your way through life or to give you a job because you need to get out and get retrained, pursue certain skills that you have because this plant is not going to care whether you've got them or not. You've got to do what you have to do. It doesn't even necessarily mean talent—just pursue some other interest. Pursue a different way of life or pursue something that you enjoy or something that's going to make you a living because don't rest on that company to bank on the rest of your life because it's not going to happen. I mean, I thought I was going to retire from there, I really did. We all did because we all thought that way. And when you think that a place is never going to close you better reevaluate what it's all about because it's not going to happen. That's why I say, just get reeducated, retrained, just pursue other interests because it's not going to be there.

I think it's [job security] gone. Everybody is so individualistic—everybody is out for themselves. There's no such thing as people working together for a common cause anymore. I mean, I don't see it. I wish I would. I would love to work for a place like that. I don't care if it's union, nonunion—of course, I'm a totally union person. Always will be all my life—but we wouldn't have to worry about unions and all these things going on if people would just have a little common sense, common courtesy. Forget about greed, let's just work for the common cause. We're all out here together; we're all out here for, we have to eat and we have to breathe and all this kind of stuff and the only way to do it is you got to go out there and make a living; why can't we work together? But it's not going to happen.

It's just I've seen it so much—the climate from the day we started in that plant to today. I've been sheltered in that surroundings all these years and never seen nothing, but since I've been out the last two years it's terrible—it's just unbelievable. I've never seen anything like it. I've talked to people in construction sites and all these people and every one of them said that they wished they could quit tomorrow but they can't because they have to pay the bills. They have to pay for the family, the kids go to school, clothing, and all this stuff. But they hate it—they hate it. They're working their butts, some of them working their butts off, and pipe fitters and drywall people and all these kind of people and you wouldn't believe it. And I said, "Gosh." Everybody is in a terrible frame of mind until Friday comes when you know it's weekend time and they're getting their paycheck, and they feel better about it.

Danny Mann, Johnson Controls

I don't care what kind of job Cody [his son] gets; what I want him to do is to get the education. If you don't want the education, if you can't cut college, if you don't want to go to college, go to the service or get you a trade. Preferably the second, get you a trade.

Thomas Rhodes, International Harvester

I think from the period of the long strike we learned a lot of lessons, or I did. I say we, my wife and I together. We always pretty much spent not everything we made but we didn't save probably half as much as we should have. We didn't live way above our means. By no means were we in debt severely other than car payments or something like that. Of course, we had a house payment but that was not a real serious nature since she worked and it was low enough that we could still make the payments and maintain our home and things. But I guess I had always put too much faith in the company. After I saw really how they did and what happened during that strike and everything that was involved in it and how easy it would be to lose everything, I never ever trusted them with my own personal welfare again. Never. And never would. I mean if I was still working I wouldn't.

I think you learn a lot from things like that, after losing the job and realizing yeah, it can happen. By the time I got around [to looking] the jobs were pretty much gone because the people that got laid off prior to me not only in my plant but in Seagrams and Brown & Williamson and all these other places we talked about earlier—things were happening there too, and those jobs were being diminished and done away with. You had a lot of people in a kind of "damned if you do, damned if you don't" situation. The way we had our seniority set up, which I think is probably a lot like a lot of people's, but we also had a program called SUB, Supplemental Unemployment Benefits [sup-pay or sub-pay]. It allowed people with over a year's service to draw up to a year's or 60 percent of what they would have made up to a year. People are laid off because of their junior seniority, not their seniority that was a little more senior. So by the time it got to us, the sub-pay had pretty well depleted, and most of the decent jobs around town were gone.

So, you're out in the cold basically. I drew ten weeks of sub at sixty dollars a week, and at that time I should have been drawing over $500.00. But it had gotten so low to where it was down to a point of being only ten weeks instead of fifty-two, and that's all I ever got out of it in all the years I worked there. I never got a penny out of it other than that. Of course, I was never laid off so I don't begrudge it. I don't begrudge the program—what I begrudge is what the company did, and I feel like they did that to put us all in that kind of position. I don't know if you're aware of it or not but there was no one from this plant in Louisville or the foundry that ever went to work at any of the other Harvester plants from a management standpoint. Nobody. Now, there are some that came from the other plants that were in Springfield and Indianapolis but there's nobody from Louisville.

Do I see the company or other companies, especially the company that I worked for, in my opinion do people wrong? Yeah, I think they can and do today—very much so. And I think personally if there was ever a need for unions in this country it's probably greater today than it was twenty years ago. I don't think people have woken up to the realization of that yet and maybe never will, I don't know. But I think they could and should. Because in my opinion we are really being sold down the river in this country.

I think they [the government] play a severe role in it in allowing it. And I don't mean literally. By allowing it, I mean more so by encouraging it than the permission of such. All during the Reagan years corporations were given U.S. tax dollars to relocate and help supposedly start Third World nations into a prosperous future with your tax dollars and mine, or your mother and daddy's or whomever. I think it's wrong, and I think they played a severe role in it. Because there's no way that we as Americans will really benefit from this. You may benefit in the technical industries and things for awhile but sooner or later they're going to eat your lunch. They're going to eat your lunch, and then what happens? Who pays for these other jobs? Who pays the taxes? Who pays for the services? Who helps pay your salary? .... Who wins? If there's nobody—it's not just factories that are closing down. Have you noticed that? It was factories to start with but now it's getting into the educated people's jobs.

And where does it stop? Who stops it? The government certainly isn't trying to. Hell, they're encouraging it. Trying to open it up even more today. And corporations are certainly not opposed to it. They're not only in line behind it but they're flipping dollar bills out just as fast as they can to get it. So who's going to win? Do you think they're going to bring all this money back to the United States and help support you and me and all these other millions of people when they're making the product somewhere else? No. It ain't going to happen. If it does it'll sure surprise me. I'll have to see it to believe it. I don't think it's going to happen. I think we're going to end up as a nation that is much, much different and much less affluent than we've ever been in our history. I really do. And I hope to God I'm wrong but I don't think it's true. And to me it scares me because that's something I can't do anything to control. That's the type of thing that bothers me.

I've told Tate [his son] that and he thinks I'm crazy, that things will be fine and technology and all this stuff today, that it's just a joke, it won't happen. Says I worry too much about conspiracies and that type of thing. I'm not really so much a conspirator or conspiratous, I think my brother tends to be that way a whole lot and maybe somewhat justifiable. But I think I'm certainly not as much as he is. But I think that there are things that could and should be done in this country from the standpoint of its citizens and its workforce. Because in my opinion manufacturing and production type jobs may not be the answer to all sins or all evils or all the greatest things but I think without a certain amount of them...everybody's not a doctor or a lawyer. They don't have the potential or the desire or anything else to be. Now, we're even going to have a serious, severe situation with welfare and people that have-not in this country, and what does that lead to?

Rob McQueen, International Harvester

God, I could never go back to work in a factory, not myself personally. Assembly lines and stuff like that—it's completely different from the average job. They have you every minute of that eight and a half hours that you're there. When that line stops, you take your ten-minute break, and you better be back when that line starts moving or you're behind, and you just mess up the whole damn thing. Oh Lord, I wouldn't wish that on my worst enemy. Of course, there's good money, and there's security and stuff, but there is no way I could go back to that. No way and I guess that's why I never tried once I got this job—it doesn't pay that much, have a lot of peace of mind with it. I'm outside. I just could never envision myself going back to something like that.

Phil Nalley, International Harvester

Well, it's turned out positive. I know that there was a period of time I was resentful of any management person. I want to use another word but I can't think of it—I was antimanagement, yes. I feel sorry for some of the people that I did work for, because as I went to work at some of these other places and I learned the contracts, and I held them to the letter of the law. And I made some of their lives not as good as it could have been. Recognizing that this did nothing but hurt me, more or less, because I was the one that was mad all the time, I eased off. It made me wiser, less trusting, and it kind of proves today in corporate America that you are a number. You're not really within a lot of companies—some do take a general interest in their people, but that you can't depend on the company—as my father knew it—you can't depend on that any longer. And also, you need to be aware of what's going on outside around you. If an opportunity presents itself that would be better, don't stay just because that's what you knew happened. You went to work one place, you stayed there, and you retired, and got the gold watch and went on.

I think it really opened my eyes up to change—that change isn't all that bad, that it can be very positive. I'm not afraid of change. I deal with it daily at work for something new either in technology or the new doctors that come in. I maintain the ORs [operating rooms at a hospital] and so I get to see a lot of stuff in those areas—and with the construction, just change of the physical plant and ... it's every day. I know a lot of people and one of the guys I work with, he just hates it when something changes. And I talk to him, "You need to ... don't worry about that stuff; it's just something different you do tomorrow. That's all it is." So yeah, I think it actually, overall, had a very positive ending. Sure, I would have loved to retire after twenty-five years. Retiring to me doesn't mean stop working. It means just stop what I'm doing now to find something I want to do later. And we were talking about that today that yeah, I would like to—I don't know whether it'll be volunteer work or work at Walgreens ... I want to do something because I can't see myself sitting at home. Traveling is fun to a point, but then you can't travel all the time either and I'm a firm believer of balance, that you have to maintain that. What better way to get out and meet new people or see different things outside of your home?

Conclusion

As listeners, readers, fellow citizens, and scholars, what are the most important lessons we can learn from these narrators? When we began recording the stories of former Harvester and Johnson Controls employees, our primary questions were what caused the closings and how were the workers' lives affected. These concerns grew out of our reading of the literature on plant closings, which documented both the national phenomenon of deindustrialization and case studies of the process in specific industries or communities. We sought to augment this scholarship by presenting fuller stories from the workers in their own words. We anticipated filling in the "other side of the story" of the causes of the closings and conveying a more detailed and personal picture of the results.

From these interviews, besides gaining insight about the impact of deindustrialization on individuals, we learn the value of oral history for providing access not just to the "firsthand" details of experience but the workers' interpretation of why and how the closing happened and what it meant for them and for society. At times the stories we heard surprised us by contradicting our expectations based on the literature on deindustrialization. What was most interesting was not just what the narrators said but how they said it: their choice of topics to emphasize and the way they grappled to make meaning of their stories. They produced an interpretation of their own story and of the history of their workplace that highlighted their skill and agency, justified an expectation of respect, and conveyed their profound sense of resentment and alienation when businesses failed to pay it. With their interpretation of events they helped us not only to see the plant closing from the inside but more important to understand it as a factor shaping contemporary working-class ideology and culture.

By their very nature, individual life and work stories are shaped by time, circumstances, and personality. As a result, any collection of personal narratives will contain a great range of experiences and points of view, reflecting the diversity of human life. Scholars working with such a body of evidence thus should be wary of making overgeneralizations and should instead respect the uniqueness of each story. Among this set of narrators, although most were white, male, and working class, there were people who were long past retirement age and others who were still in their peak working years. The former, such as Charlie Noyes, had long histories of work experience to draw from to contextualize the events of the closing, and the option of retiring rather than seeking new employment. Some were loquacious and charismatic, eager to talk and welcoming; others were more hesitant, taciturn, and private. A few exuded optimism and self-assurance, like Bob Reed seeing each change in life as an opportunity. Others were more discouraged and even frightened by the loss of insurance and other benefits and the uncertainty of whether their health would hold out until retirement age. While most of the narrators claimed to have been able to predict the closing, or at least to know it was going to happen for a while, a few expressed more surprise. This was the case for one or two workers at Harvester who declared they just could not believe a plant such as that could be shut down until near the very end.

For scholars of deindustrialization, the benefit of the diversity of these life histories is that they provide evidence for the complexity of the story. Although there are myriad common themes in the interviews regarding how the workers at the two plants described their jobs, explained the closings and assessed the impact, there are also some divergences, indicating the case-specific nature of some aspects of the deindustrialization story. In the popular imagination, a plant closing happens in an instant; employees go to work to find the factory shuttered and their lives devastated. In these stories it is clear that closings can be a protracted and complicated affair, at times taking years, and that each follows its own course. At Harvester, the process began in 1982 with the first of a series of layoffs and sell-offs of divisions, and ended when the forge shop changed hands in 1985. During that time individual workers could find themselves laid off, recalled, and moved to other jobs in the plant due to the seniority system that allowed longer-term employees to bump or "roll" others. This prolonged uncertainty disrupted searches for other employment and contributed to the tension surrounding the closing. The experience of the plant closing could also extend long after the doors shut, as some employees took advantage of recall rights to go to company facilities elsewhere—stretching their involvement with Harvester in some cases for years. While the closing of Johnson Controls did not take quite as long, there was a buildup of anxiety as rumors flew about whether the Louisville facility would be one of the plants to go, and as employees were led to believe if they improved production they would be spared. Because few took the company up on its offer to relocate them—to other plants with no seniority benefits—for most Johnson Controls employees the experience was shorter and often more intense, creating, as is evidenced by the interviews, more animosity toward the company.

The two cases also enable us to view some difference in the political and union response to the closings. According to the narrators, coming at the time of the early 1980s recession and Reagan-era hostility to unions, the closing of Harvester elicited nothing but disinterest from local, state, and national officials. As one narrator recalled, "We didn't get any help from anybody." In fact, some accused city leaders of animosity toward the plant and the heavy industry it represented. On the other hand, Harvester workers expressed ardent appreciation and support for their union, explicitly confronting the popular mythology that well-paid union employees were the cause of deindustrialization. Even those few narrators who thought the union could have been more flexible defended it and insisted it was not the cause of the shutdown. By the mid-1990s national government, because of the adoption of NAFTA, was seen as not just indifferent but as an enemy of working-class concerns, and was blamed for the closing. But, in the latter case, state and city officials, worried about the loss of local jobs as waves of capital flight continued to affect even the low-wage southern region, worked hard to keep Johnson Controls open and in Kentucky. This same national/local split is seen in descriptions of union officials' actions. Narrators praised their local union for trying to protect them, displaying the same loyalty to it as seen at Harvester. But they expressed disappointment in national officers who, in this case in the interest of preserving the union's strength in remaining plants, were willing to sacrifice benefits in Louisville. Thus, while the interviews by their nature focus on individuals' stories, they provide evidence about the larger political context and how it changed, and in some ways did not change, in this period.

On the more personal level, the narratives also reveal that the impact of deindustrialization depended on life circumstances, which were unique for each person. Some workers talked about being cushioned by wives with good-paying jobs, a factor that also could make taking advantage of recall rights more complicated and less appealing. Those whose children were grown felt grateful for having one less burden, while others with young children were constrained in what alternate employment they were willing to seek. In some cases health problems limited the choice of future jobs, or for others enabled early medical retirement as in the case of both Rhodes brothers. For a few, personal or family health problems made the closing in part a relief, as when Marilyn Reed feared she couldn't take the heavy labor much longer or when Winfred Shake recalled having more time to spend with his wife during her illness. The idiosyncratic elements of each story remind us of the true value of oral history, that it illuminates how any experience, in this case the impact of deindustrialization on workers, is both informed by and understood through the context of life circumstances.

Nevertheless, for all the distinctiveness of the content of each life story, a remarkable consistency in certain emphases, themes, and motifs arises from the body of interviews, producing a shared story and interpretation of these events. Despite differences in the process of the two closings, most of the narrators agreed in general terms on who or what was the cause of the shutdown. They shifted blame away from stubborn unions (a common target for popular and press censure at the time), onerous regulation, or even broad and amorphous economic conditions, and toward poor decisions on the part of company management. While admitting that other businesses were having a hard time and closing in the same era, these narrators maintained that particular actions doomed these plants. Harvester stopped making the Scout and missed out on the SUV craze. Johnson Controls paid too little attention to quality and lost the Sears contract. Although at times the narrators attributed these mistakes to simple mismanagement, often they linked them to more nefarious motives such as the breaking of the union and the desire for profits that would come from shipping jobs abroad. In the workers' memory, McCardell pledged to break the Harvester unions and Johnson Controls executives targeted the most organized plants. In the latter case, the narrators argued that as a result of NAFTA companies could more easily attack unions because they had the recourse—and thus the threat—of taking the jobs and leaving.

The narrators in this collection were very clear about one factor that did not cause the closings: an inability or failure on the part of the workers themselves. Instead they insisted that the quality of the work never declined and that the employees did everything they could to keep the plants open and successful. This perspective reflects a broader theme that dominated the interviews: the skill and hard work of the employees, especially in nearly unbearable conditions. In these conversations we learn more about the hazards of the work done in these factories than any other topic. Again and again the narrators returned to the subject of the dangers of extreme heat, molten iron, lead dust, and accidents. These vivid depictions help the listener and reader to understand day-to-day life inside a major production facility. But more important, the insistence on these topics reveals what the narrators believe the future audience must understand: working in these factories was hell. This "fact" sets up the most important lessons they try to convey, that only a certain kind of person has the skill and determination to do this kind of work, they ought to be respected for it, and that they are better off since the plants closed.[1]

The narrators painted graphic pictures of the perilous nature of their workplaces and the arduousness of their jobs as a backdrop for emphasizing their personal skill and ability to take it. They attributed their work ethic and endurance to their blue-collar backgrounds and the lessons they learned from their fathers about doing a fair day's work for a fair day's pay. Like Danny Mann and Rob McQueen, they told stories about how they and a few close coworkers were strong enough and smart enough to master their tasks better than others. As a result they were dependable employees who were praised by their superiors and considered leaders by their peers. Not only were they survivors who could stand the heat and pressure, they recognized problems in the plants that the managers did not or could not. Charlie Noyes and others, for example, witnessed the impact of poor maintenance as a source of trouble, and Marilyn Reed from her perspective in quality control could foresee the decline of the Johnson Controls facility. These insights led them to declare, in varying terms but with the same meaning, that they "saw it coming"—the closing of the plant—before management knew it or admitted it. Because of this insight, they were able to prepare themselves and their families and thus avoid the worst of the impacts of unemployment, something their less fortunate or less prescient colleagues could not do. To their listener and the imagined broader audience, then, these narrators portrayed themselves as agents whose skill contributed to the company's success and kept them from being victims of its downfall.

The workers expected more than just high pay and job security in return for that skill, hard work, and willingness to endure dangerous conditions; they expected respect. The narrators often concede that they were well paid, though they add that their salaries resulted in large part from the efforts of the union and that they should be compensated considering what they put up with. But, their critique of their employers reveals they believed they did not get the respect they were due, expressed most often in their indignation over, put most simply, not being treated right. They felt management lied to them, misled them about the future of the plants, cheated them out of due benefits. They asserted they had been treated like a disposable machine part or "just a number" rather than as a person who devoted long hours and considerable effort to the success of the business. This view contributed to the sense of alienation expressed when asked what they had learned from their experiences. They saw no loyalty on the part of managers, and no commitment to them as workers. They were as disgruntled with government, whose leaders were indifferent or hostile to the fate of the working class, willing to facilitate shipping their jobs overseas, and lowering the standard of living for all. In short, no one in power gave them the respect and consideration they felt they were due. These narratives thus suggest not only what working-class men and women of the late 1960s through 1990s expected from and endured for their jobs and the pride they felt in their ability and in what they built; they also convey the resentment and loss of trust by those who felt betrayed and disrespected by their employers and government. In doing so they reveal one factor contributing to the alienation of such working men and women from politics, their workplaces, and investment and true equal participation in American economic life.

Although the narrators focused on their own story and on conveying their personal experience to future audiences, the interviews also contain commentary of a more communal and societal nature. Narrators broke from their personal experience to comment upon what happened to others—often in a comparative frame—and the social and economic results of deindustrialization for the country. The former employees of Harvester and Johnson Controls passed along stories about coworkers who lost marriages, cars, and homes, or who had health crises brought out by the stress of unemployment. Howard Etherton, in his role as benefits representative, shared information about the consequences for some workers. But, in most of the interviews these stories came out as part of a critique of others who lived "high on the hog" or were not smart enough to foresee the closing. They used their less fortunate former colleagues as a foil to assert their own agency and lack of victimhood. Despite the judgmental tone, however, the content still provides evidence for, and demonstrates concern about, some of the more negative impacts on the community. Moreover, when asked to draw lessons from the experience, the narrators returned repeatedly to concern about the direction of the economy and the nation. They blamed NAFTA for dragging down workplace conditions and the standard of living for blue-collar people like themselves. They feared a polarization in the country and dire results from that ranging from an increase in drug use and violence to a loss of constitutional freedoms. Most importantly and most commonly, they bemoaned the loss of security that future generations will suffer. In this vein, though they emphasized individual agency, they also indicated a social concern not just for their own children but for working-class people and even the nation as a whole.

Perhaps the most surprising thing we learn from these narrators is that quite a number of them felt they are better off than they were before the closing. Nearly every individual described negative consequences of the closing for themselves and others. They experienced steep declines in income, they gave up or postponed treasured retirement plans, and they saw their standard of living drop. Yet most of them also listed the ways in which they are happier. Most important, they were at the time of the interviews healthier than they would have been if they were still in the plants. Rob McQueen no longer woke up with metal dust in his eyes, Marilyn Reed did not suffer from muscle and joint pain. Further, several of the narrators expected to live longer as a result of their changed work lives. Moreover, many of them bragged that in their new jobs they have more room for creativity and more chance to use their minds. Several of them are employed doing maintenance for schools, churches, and hospitals and they appreciate the variety of the work and the ingenuity required. Others valued the autonomy, especially the ability to make their own schedules. In short, they felt more in control of their work lives and health. Finally, they claimed to be treated better by employers who know them and appreciate them. Their stories of what pleases them about their new jobs shed light on the dreams and desires of not only these individuals but, perhaps, workers more broadly—autonomy, the chance to be creative, and appreciation.

From an oral history perspective the most intriguing aspect of this project was recording the narrators' efforts to reconcile this happy ending they feel they have reached with evidence to the contrary and their expressed concern about the dire economic future they see for their families and the nation as well as their resentment and anger over the treatment they received from management. The struggle to do so produced narratives that are full of ambivalence. At times interviewees made contradictory statements within a story or narrative. A common device was "book ending," that is, starting a story with a positive assertion, including evidence of negative experience, but concluding on an upbeat note. For example one narrator began "It wasn't that stressful on me," described at length his decline in income, then ended with "None of that affected me." In a few cases, the workers quite explicitly acknowledged their internal conflict over these issues, with Rob McQueen even granting that "whoever listens to this will think I'm nuts," because he could not settle on whether the plant closing was positive or negative for him.

Faced with these contradictions it would be easy to conclude that the narrators, in trying to promote a positive self-image, distort the full negative impact of what happened to them. But, such a "false consciousness" interpretation is patronizing to the narrators and fails to recognize the complexity and richness oral history brings to the study of the problem of plant closings. Indeed, these complicated and often internally contradictory narratives reveal that experience is never simple or unidimensional. First, we learn that the process and results of a plant closing are more knotty than straightforward. These narrators described a long, drawn-out process of decisions and responses and of layoffs and recalls that belies the image of a sudden announcement and shutdown. They viewed the plant closings and their causes in the context of a longer story, often stretching back for years before the key events and, because of seniority-based call backs to other facilities of the same company, lasting for years after the local factory shut down.

More important, these complicated and sometimes contradictory narratives remind us that people, like experiences, are complex and can hold multiple values and have many reactions at once.[2] While unhappy with some aspects of their jobs, the narrators recognized that they were well compensated, felt satisfaction in being able to do their tasks well, and had been enmeshed in a supportive community of fellow workers. But, they also dreamed of a different future and many of them in retrospect saw that the closing freed them to pursue it. In short, they could be depressed and happy, resentful and grateful at the same time. They may not have yet fully integrated their conflicting emotions. Thus, by giving the narrators the time to describe their paradoxical reactions, oral history adds to the story of deindustrialization the complexity of human experience.

Timeline

International Harvester

1946	International Harvester acquired land and existing plant facilities in Louisville.
1973	Labor force reached 6,800 across the 3 Louisville facilities (assembly plant, forge, and foundry).
Late 1970s	Labor force reduced to 2,500. Reductions began with the decline of farm equipment sales.
November 1979–May 1980	Workers in Louisville participated in UAW strike against the company, referred to as the "six-months strike."
Early 1980s	International Harvester reported business losses.
July 29, 1982	The company announced the first closure at Louisville facility.
January 1983	The assembly plant closed.
August 1984	The foundry closed.
April 1985	The forge closed.

Johnson Controls

1978	Johnson Controls expanded its operations to include automotive batteries by acquiring Globe Union.
April 1994	Johnson Controls announced loss of major contract to produce DieHard batteries for Sears.
Late 1994	Louisville plant management and union officials learned that their plant is included in a list of potential closures. Workers requested to find ways (e.g., improving production) to increase likelihood that plant will remain open.
April 1995	The company announced decision to close the Louisville plant.
October 1995	Company financials revealed $67 million in income.
December 1995	The Louisville plant closed.

Narrators

Don Anderson

Anderson grew up in Louisville with a love of making things work and a desire to go into the electrical field. He worked briefly for Link Electric and received training as an electrician in the Navy and in trade school. After a few years of employment with L&N railroad, in 1964 he got a job in maintenance at International Harvester. When Harvester closed its doors twenty-two years later, he took an electronics course, did some television and radio repair, and then got a job doing maintenance for a local Catholic parish school.

Howard Etherton

For Etherton, working at International Harvester ran in the family. His father started there shortly after it opened, in 1947. Etherton joined the Army at seventeen and after he was discharged worked briefly for Pepsi-Cola and General Electric. Then in 1957 he and his brother, following in their dad's footsteps, went to work at Harvester. Later, he became a union official and when Harvester closed its doors he moved into full-time employment dealing with retiree and transfer benefits for the UAW.

Danny Mann

Mann grew up in Louisville after his parents moved the family there when he was a child. In high school he went to work at Kroger, but when his manager would not let him transfer to a higher-paid department he went to Ford Motor Company. After layoffs at Ford he looked for a more secure industry and bet on Johnson Controls. When the plant closed he moved through a number of lower-paid, nonunionized jobs as he tried to avoid going back into industrial work, then settled into employment in maintenance at the Home of the Innocents, a local home for orphans and foster children.

Rob McQueen

McQueen was born in 1952 and raised in Louisville. After getting married in high school he worked at Louisville Ladder and then Ralston-Purina before moving to International Harvester in 1973 for better pay. After the Harvester closing he made a living in a number of short-term jobs before settling down with the Metro Parks Department.

Phil Nalley

Born in Louisville in 1950, Nalley attended local Catholic schools and then a vocational high school. After graduation he worked in welding at the Marley Company, then in 1973 went to work at International Harvester for the better pay and benefits. After he was laid off from Harvester he worked as a custodian for a Catholic school, and for a short time for a local defense manufacturer, before starting a job doing maintenance for Jewish Hospital.

Charlie Noyes

Charlie Noyes grew up in the Louisville area, on both sides of the Ohio River. He started working in high school for auto dealerships and body shops. He tried to get an apprenticeship as a machinist, but when he was unable to he took a job at American Tobacco. He worked there seventeen years, then went through his first plant closing. When that company shut down in January 1971, he moved to the maintenance department at Globe Union. When Johnson Controls, which had purchased Globe Union, announced it too was closing, he took early retirement to try to save the younger men a few months of work.

Ron Phillips

Phillips was born and raised in Louisville, where his father worked for International Harvester. When he graduated high school he intended to go to college at Western Kentucky University, but was drafted. After serving in Vietnam from 1969 to 1971, he returned to Louisville and got a job at Globe Union. When the company, which had become Johnson Controls, closed he turned down a chance to transfer to a facility in another state and got a job doing service on recreational vehicles.

Roy Puckett

Puckett moved to Louisville as a child with his family and grew up in the south end of town. After high school he worked as a mechanic for a car dealership and then at the Wood Mosaic company before a relative helped him in 1971 get a job that paid better at Globe Union. In 1989 he became an official with the local union and served in that capacity in addition to his production work until the plant closed. After Johnson Controls shut down, he sought retraining but then was offered a job doing maintenance for the UAW union hall.

Arthur "Buddy" Pugh

Born in 1943, Pugh grew up in a rural area south of Louisville where his father farmed. After high school he went to work at a local distillery, and then his brother got him a job at Johnson Controls because the pay was better. Later, after Johnson Controls closed he went to work for Publisher's Printing doing construction and maintenance.

Bob Reed

Reed's father was a traveling salesman who moved the family around the country, leaving him wanting a settled life in a steady field. In high school he considered art school, but in his senior year when his father died he began a series of short-term jobs. Needing more money and better pay in 1972 he settled at Globe Union. When he lost his job in the closing of Johnson Controls, Reed went back to his original dream and pursued making art for a living.

Marilyn Reed

Born in 1946, Reed grew up in Louisville's west end, where her father had a bakery. After high school she got a job as a secretary, but quit when she married and moved to Japan with her husband who was stationed there with the military. In 1971, after her divorce, her sister-in-law got her a job in the Johnson Controls customer service and then payroll department. She then moved into the production end of the plant, working several jobs there until the closing. After Johnson Controls shut down she took advantage of dislocated-worker retraining programs and went back into payroll and office work.

Mike Reid

Reid was born in Louisville in 1958. After a short stint working for his father, who was a plumber, and at a cabinet-making company, he began work at Johnson Controls in April 1979. After the closing he went into refrigeration and air conditioning repair.

Frank Reinhart

Reinhart was born and raised in the south end of Louisville. After working at the police station part-time and at Pepsi-Cola, at age twenty-two he went to work for Johnson Controls. After management announced the closing of the plant he resigned due to illness. Because of his medical disability, unrelated to his work at Johnson Controls, he has only been employed occasionally since the shutdown.

Kenneth "Kenny" Rhodes

Rhodes grew up in Louisville, the son of a truck driver. At age thirteen he got his first job at a gas station, and stayed there until 1968 when at eighteen he followed his brother Thomas into International Harvester. When he was laid off during the closing he did a number of jobs including driving a truck and working in dispatch and managerial positions related to trucking. He was recalled due to his seniority and secured a position in Indianapolis at a Harvester plant, by then called Navistar. After two years, however, health problems forced him to retire.

Thomas Rhodes

Thomas Rhodes started his work career at the same gas station as his brother. He got married and had a child in high school, so as soon as he graduated he looked for a better-paying job and went with some friends to International Harvester. When he was laid off during the closing he worked briefly part-time for the United Way, then got his real estate license. Like his brother, he got called to a Navistar plant; this one in Springfield, Ohio. He worked there for eight years, commuting back and forth to Louisville, until heart problems led him to take medical retirement.

Winfred Shake

Shake moved with his family to Louisville in 1938 when his father began working for Superior Petroleum, and grew up in south Louisville. He started working at age sixteen for a grocery store. After a number of other jobs and a stint in the service during World War II he started work at International Harvester in 1947, shortly after it opened. When he saw the trouble the company was in by the early 1980s he retired early to avoid being caught in layoffs.

Notes

Introduction

1. Barry Bluestone and Bennett Harrison, *The Deindustrialization of America: Plant Closings, Community Abandonment, and the Dismantling of Basic Industry* (New York: Basic Books, Inc., 1982).

2. Michael Wallace and Joyce Rothschild, "Plant Closings, Capital Flight, and Worker Dislocation: The Long Shadow of Deindustrialization," in *Deindustrialization and the Restructuring of American Industry*, ed. Michael Wallace and Joyce Rothschild (Greenwich, CT: JAI Press, 1988), 1–35; Kenneth Root, "Job Loss: Whose Fault, What Remedies?" in *Deindustrialization and the Restructuring of American Industry*, 65–84; Terry F. Buss and C. Richard Hofstetter, "Powerlessness, Anomie, and Cynicism: The Personal Consequences of Mass Unemployment in a Steel Town," *Micropolitics* 2 (1983): 349–377; Terry F. Buss and R. Stevens Redburn, *Shutdown at Youngstown: Public Policy for Mass Unemployment* (Albany, NY: State University of New York Press, 1983); Clifford L. Broman, V. Lee Hamilton, and William S. Hoffman, "Unemployment and Its Effects on Families: Evidence from a Plant Closing Study," *American Journal of Community Psychology* 18 (1990): 643–659.

3. Michael Frisch, "Oral History and the Presentation of Class Consciousness: The *New York Times* v. The Buffalo Unemployed," in *A Shared Authority: Essays on the Craft and Meaning of Oral and Public History* (Albany, NY: State University of New York Press, 1990), 59–80.

4. David Bensman and Roberta Lynch, *Rusted Dreams: Hard Times in a Steel Community* (New York: McGraw-Hill, 1987); Kathryn Marie Dudley, *The End of the Line: Lost Jobs, New Lives in Postindustrial America* (Chicago, IL: University of Chicago Press, 1994); Steven High, *Industrial Sunset: The Making of North American's Rust Belt, 1969–1984* (Toronto: University of Toronto Press, 2003); Sherry Lee Linkon and John Russo, *Steeltown USA: Work and Memory in Youngstown* (Lawrence, KS: University Press of Kansas, 2002). For other examples

see Gregory Pappas, *The Magic City: Unemployment in a Working Class Community* (Ithaca, NY: Cornell University Press, 1989); Jefferson Cowie, *Capital Moves: RCA's Seventy-Year Quest for Cheap Labor* (New York: The New Press, 2001). On the theme of memory or use of oral history to document worker experience, see, e.g., John Bodnar, "Power and Memory in Oral History: Workers and Managers at Studebaker," *Journal of American History* 75 (1989): 1201–1221; Steve May and Laura Morrison, "Making Sense of Restructuring: Narratives of Accommodation among Downsized Workers," in *Beyond the Ruins: The Meanings of Deindustrialization*, ed. Jefferson Cowie and Joseph Heathcott (Ithaca, NY: Cornell University Press, 2003), 259–283.

5. Michael Frisch, *Portraits in Steel* with photographs by Milton Rogovin (Ithaca, NY: Cornell University Press, 1993); Thomas Dublin, *When the Mines Closed: Stories of Struggles in Hard Times* with photographs by George Harvan (Ithaca, NY: Cornell University Press, 1998).

6. Judith Modell and Charlee Brodsky, *Town without Steel: Envisioning Homestead* (Pittsburgh, PA: University of Pittsburgh Press, 1998); Steven High and David W. Lewis, *Corporate Wasteland: The Landscape and Memory of Deindustrialization* (Ithaca, NY: Cornell University Press, 2007); Cedric N. Chatterley, Alicia J. Rouverol, and Stephen A. Cole, *"I Was Content and Not Content": The Story of Linda Lord and the Closing of Penobscot Poultry* (Carbondale, IL: Southern Illinois University Press, 2000). A similar example is Bill Bamberger and Cathy N. Davidson, *Closing: The Life and Death of an American Factory* (New York: W. W. Norton, 1998). In this case, however, the authors retell the workers' stories rather than present interview text.

7. On the nature of oral history as evidence see Michael Frisch, "Oral History and Hard Times," in *A Shared Authority*, 5–14; Alessandro Portelli, "What Makes Oral History Different," in *The Death of Luigi Trastulli and Other Stories: Form and Meaning in Oral History* (Albany, NY: State University of New York Press, 1991), 45–58; Ronald J. Grele, "Oral History as Evidence," in *Handbook of Oral History*, ed. Thomas L. Charlton, Lois E. Myers, and Rebecca Sharpless (New York: Altamira Press, 2006), 43–101.

8. John Portz, *The Politics of Plant Closings* (Lawrence, KS: University Press of Kansas, 1990).

9. George C. Yater, *Two Hundred Years at the Falls of the Ohio: A History of Louisville and Jefferson County* (Louisville, KY: Heritage Corporation of Louisville and Jefferson County, 1979), 101, 155, 175–180.

10. Ibid., 195, 199, 201, 206–210; Richard Bernier, "World War II," in *Encyclopedia of Louisville*, ed. John Kleber et al. (Lexington, KY: University Press of Kentucky, 2001), 954–957.

11. "Louisville: A Blend of Almost Everywhere," *Business Week*, May 7, 1955; Census figures from *Census of the Population: 1960, Vol. 1: Characteristics of the Population, Part 19, KY* (Washington, DC: U.S. Department of Commerce, 1963) and *1970 Census of Population, Vol. 1: Characteristics of the Population, Part 19, KY* (Washington, DC: U.S. Department of Commerce, 1973); Yater, *Two Hundred Years*, 221; "International Harvester Buys Curtiss Plant," *Courier Journal*, March 23, 1946; "Battery Factory to Be Built Here," *Courier Journal*, January 1, 1956; Kenneth P. Vinsel, " 'Home Grown' Industry Leads Growth of City," *Courier Journal*, January 1, 1956. For more information on the Louisville economy in the 1960s and 1970s, see "Louisville Business Trends," Louisville Area Chamber of Commerce Research Department, 1975; "Industrial Resources: Louisville, Kentucky," Louisville Chamber of Commerce and the Kentucky Department of Commerce, 1967; "Survey, Analysis and Forecast: The Economic Base and Population, Metropolitan Louisville," Louisville and Jefferson County Planning and Zoning Commission, 1964.
12. Portz, *The Politics of Plant Closings*, 37–52.
13. These interviews were transcribed according to the model used for all Oral History Center interviews. That model is loosely based on the one presented by Willa Baum in *Transcribing and Editing Oral History* (Walnut Creek, CA: AltaMira, 1995), with some revisions over the years. In brief, these are nearly verbatim accounts with vocal ticks and stutter sentence fragments eliminated for ease of reader comprehension.
14. On the concept of shared authority, see Michael Frisch, "Introduction," in *A Shared Authority*, xv–xxiv.
15. Barbara Allen, "Story in Oral History: Clues to Historical Consciousness," *Journal of American History* 79 (1992): 606–611; Samuel Schrager, "What Is Social in Oral History," *International Journal of Oral History* 4 (1983): 76–98; Alicia J. Rouverol, "Retelling the Story of Linda Lord," in *"I Was Content and Not Content,"* 117–131.

I   "This Plant's Going to Be There Forever"

1. For information on the Louisville economy in this period, see "Louisville Business Trends," Louisville Area Chamber of Commerce Research Department, 1975; "Industrial Resources: Louisville, Kentucky," Louisville Chamber of Commerce and the Kentucky Department of Commerce, 1967; "Survey, Analysis and Forecast: The Economic Base

and Population, Metropolitan Louisville," Louisville and Jefferson County Planning and Zoning Commission, 1964.

3 "That Factory Wasn't Going to Last"

1. For the national story of Harvester's fortunes in the late 1970s and early 1980s, see Carol J. Loomis, "Strike that Rained on Archie McCardell's Parade," *Fortune*, May 19, 1980, 90–99; David Pauly with Donna M. Foote, "Harvester Faces Post-Strike Blues," *Newsweek*, June 2, 1980, 72; Carol J. Loomis, "Archie McCardell's Absolution," *Fortune*, December 15, 1980, 89–98; "Hard Times at Harvester," *Time*, May 25, 1981, 67; "Goodbye, Archie," *Time*, May 17, 1982, 57.

2. Ben Z. Hershberg and Jay Lawrence, "Harvester Slowdown Will Result in Layoffs of 1,600 in Louisville," *Courier Journal* , February 6, 1982; "GE, Harvester Set Summer Shutdowns," *Courier Journal*, June 18, 1982; Ben Z. Hershberg, "Harvester May Close Some of Plant Temporarily," *Courier Journal*, July 13, 1982; Ben Z. Hershberg, "International Harvester to Close Plant," *Courier Journal*, July 30, 1982; "Harvester to Begin Shutting Down Plant by End of Month," *Courier Journal*, September 3, 1982; "Harvester Exploring Prospects for Foundry in Louisville," *Courier Journal*, September 30, 1982; Bob Johnson and Jay Lawrence, "Metts Exploring Rescue of Harvester Foundry," *Courier Journal*, October 9, 1982; Joe Ward, "Harvester to Close Louisville Foundry, Idling 710 Workers," *Courier Journal*, November 19, 1983; Jim Thompson, "Harvester to Sell Plant to 2 Local Businessmen," *Courier Journal*, December 12, 1984; Michael J. Upsall, "Harvester Shuts Down Last of Local Operations," *Courier Journal*, April 10, 1985.

3. For official history of Johnson Controls see http://www.johnsoncontrols.com/publish/us/en/about/history.html. The national financial press devoted very little attention to the fortunes of Johnson Controls' battery division, beyond coverage of a lawsuit against the company regarding the employment of women in the division. For information on the closing of the Louisville plant see Joe Ward, "Johnson Controls Will Stop Making DieHards When Sears Pact Runs Out," *Courier Journal*, April 24, 1994; Joe Ward, "Battery Firm Plans to Close Louisville Plant; 245 Jobs to End," *Courier Journal*, April 25, 1995; Joe Ward, "Battery Plant Closing; Area Losing 241 Jobs," *Courier Journal*, June 28, 1995.

4 "I Was Overjoyed, I Was Sad, I Was Hurt"

1. Here "sub-pay" refers to the supplemental pay given to employees at the time they lost their jobs. At times interviewees used the term sub-pay and at other times sub-pay.
2. Name withheld by request.
3. Name withheld by request.

Conclusion

1. For extended examination of these themes see Joy L. Hart and Tracy E. K'Meyer, "Worker Memory and Narrative: Personal Stories of Deindustrialization in Louisville, Kentucky," in *Beyond the Ruins: The Meanings of Deindustrialization*, ed. Jefferson Cowie and Joseph Heathcott (Ithaca, NY: Cornell University Press, 2003), 284–304.
2. For a useful discussion on this point see Frisch, "Foreword," and Rouverol, "Introduction" and "Retelling the Story of Linda Lord," all in *"I Was Content and Not Content": The Story of Linda Lord and the Closing of Penobscot Poultry* (Carbondale, IL: Southern Illinois University Press, 2000).

Bibliography

Allen, Barbara. "Story in Oral History: Clues to Historical Consciousness." *Journal of American History* 79 (1992): 606–611.

Bamberger, Bill, and Cathy N. Davidson. *Closing: The Life and Death of an American Factory.* New York: W. W. Norton, 1998.

Baum, Willa. *Transcribing and Editing Oral History.* Walnut Creek, CA: AltaMira, 1995.

Bensman, David, and Roberta Lynch. *Rusted Dreams: Hard Times in a Steel Community.* New York: McGraw-Hill, 1987.

Bluestone, Barry, and Bennett Harrison. *The Deindustrialization of America: Plant Closings, Community Abandonment, and the Dismantling of Basic Industry.* New York: Basic Books, Inc., 1982.

Bodnar, John. "Power and Memory in Oral History: Workers and Managers at Studebaker." *Journal of American History* 75 (1989): 1201–1221.

Broman, Clifford L., V. Lee Hamilton, and William S. Hoffman. "Unemployment and Its Effects on Families: Evidence from a Plant Closing Study." *American Journal Community Psychology* 18 (1990): 643–659.

Burawoy, Michael. *Manufacturing Consent: Changes in the Labor Process under Monopoly Capitalism.* Chicago, IL: University of Chicago Press, 1979.

Buss, Terry F., and F. Stevens Redburn. *Shutdown at Youngstown: Public Policy for Mass Unemployment.* Albany, NY: State University of New York Press, 1983.

Buss, Terry F., and C. Richard Hofstetter. "Powerlessness, Anomie, and Cynicism: The Personal Consequences of Mass Unemployment in a Steel Town." *Micropolitics* 2 (1988): 349–377.

Charlton, Thomas L., Lois E. Myers, and Rebecca Sharpless, eds. *Handbook of Oral History.* New York: Altamira Press, 2006.

Chatterley, Cedric N., Alicia J. Rouverol, and Stephen A. Cole. *"I Was Content and Not Content": The Story of Linda Lord and the Closing of Penobscot Poultry.* Carbondale, IL: Southern Illinois University Press, 2000.

Cochrane, Brenda. "Union Maids No More: Long-Term Impact of Loss of a Union Job on Women Workers." *Labor Studies Journal* 13 (1988): 19–34.

Cowie, Jefferson. *Capital Moves: RCA's Seventy-Year Quest for Cheap Labor.* New York: The New Press, 2001.

Cowie, Jefferson, and Joseph Heathcott, eds. *Beyond the Ruins: The Meanings of Deindustrialization*. Ithaca, NY: Cornell University Press, 2003.

Dublin, Thomas, with photographs by George Harvan. *When the Mines Closed: Stories of Struggles in Hard Times*. Ithaca, NY: Cornell University Press, 1998.

Dudley, Kathryn Marie. *The End of the Line: Lost Jobs, New Lives in Postindustrial America*. Chicago, IL: The University of Chicago Press, 1994.

Frisch, Michael. *A Shared Authority: Essays on the Craft and Meaning of Oral and Public History*. Albany, NY: State University of New York Press, 1990.

Frisch, Michael, with photographs by Milton Rogovin. *Portraits in Steel*. Ithaca, NY: Cornell University Press, 1993.

Gibson, Melissa K., and Michael J. Papa. "The Mud, the Blood, and the Beer Guys: Organizational Osmosis in Blue-Collar Work Groups." *Journal of Applied Communication Research* 28 (2000): 68–88.

High, Steven. *Industrial Sunset: The Making of North America's Rust Belt, 1969–1984*. Toronto: University of Toronto Press, 2003.

High, Steven, and David W. Lewis. *Corporate Wasteland: The Landscape and Memory of Deindustrialization*. Ithaca, NY: Cornell University Press, 2007.

Illes, Louise Moser. *Sizing Down: Chronicle of a Plant Closing*. Ithaca, NY: Cornell University Press, 1996.

"Industrial Resources: Louisville, Kentucky." Louisville Chamber of Commerce and the Kentucky Department of Commerce, 1967.

Kinicki, Angelo J. "Personal Consequences of Plant Closings: A Model and Preliminary Test." *Human Relations* 38 (1985): 197–212.

Knapp, Tim, and John Harms. "When the Screen Goes Blank: A Television Plant Closing and Its Impact on Workers." *Sociological Quarterly* 43 (2002): 607–626.

Linkon, Sherry Lee, and John Russo. *Steeltown USA: Work and Memory in Youngstown*. Lawrence, KS: University Press of Kansas, 2002.

"Louisville Business Trends." Louisville Area Chamber of Commerce Research Department, 1975.

Milkman, Ruth. *Farewell to the Factory: Autoworkers in the Late Twentieth Century*. Berkeley, CA: University of California Press, 1997.

Modell, Judith, and Charlee Brodsky. *Town without Steel: Envisioning Homestead*. Pittsburgh, PA: University of Pittsburgh Press, 1998.

Pappas, Gregory. *The Magic City: Unemployment in a Working Class Community*. Ithaca, NY: Cornell University Press, 1989.

Perrucci, Carolyn C., and Robert Perrucci. *Plant Closings: The International Context and Social Costs*. New York: Aldine De Gruyter, 1988.

Portelli, Alessandro. *The Death of Luigi Trastulli and Other Stories: Form and Meaning in Oral History*. Albany, NY: State University of New York Press, 1991.

Portz, John. *The Politics of Plant Closings.* Lawrence, KS: The University Press of Kansas, 1990.

Schrager, Samuel. "What Is Social in Oral History?" *International Journal of Oral History* 4 (1983): 76–98.

Staudohar, Paul D., and Holly E. Brown. *Deindustrialization and Plant Closure.* Lexington, MA: Lexington Books, D. C. Heath and Company, 1987.

"Survey, Analysis and Forecast: The Economic Base and Population, Metropolitan Louisville." Louisville and Jefferson County Planning and Zoning Commission, 1964.

Taylor, Shelley E., and Jonathan D. Brown. "Positive Illusions and Well-Being Revisited: Separating Fact from Fiction." *Psychological Bulletin* 116 (1994): 21–27.

Vosler, Nancy R. "Displaced Manufacturing Workers and Their Families: A Research-Based Practice Model." *Families in Society: The Journal of Contemporary Human Services* 75 (1994): 105–117.

Wallace, Michael, and Joyce Rothschild, eds. *Deindustrialization and the Restructuring of American Industry.* Greenwich, CT: JAI Press, Inc., 1988.

Periodicals

Barron's
Courier Journal
Fortune
Newsweek
Time
Wall Street Journal

Index